| BELGIUM | BELIZE | BERMUDA | BORA BORA | BRAZIL | BRITISH VIRGIN ISLANDS | BRITISH WEST INDIES | BRUNEI | BULGARIA | CAMBODIA | CANADA | CANARY ISLANDS |
GARCIA | DOMINICAN REPUBLIC | EGYPT | EL SALVADOR | ENGLAND | ERITREA | ETHIOPIA | FIJI | FRANCE | FRENCH

MW00581453

| KAZAKHSTAN | KUWAIT | KWAJALEIN ISLAND | LEBANON | LIBYA | LITHUANIA | MACAU | MACEDONIA | MALAYSIA
CALEDONIA | NEW GUINEA | NEW ZEALAND | NIGERIA | NORTHERN MARIANA ISLANDS | OMAN | PAKISTAN | PAL
H KOREA | SPAIN | SRI LANKA | ST. CROIX | ST. JOHN | ST. KITTS AND NEVIS | ST. LUCIA | ST. MARTIN | ST. THOMAS |
INE | UNITED ARAB EMIRATES | UNITED STATES OF AMERICA | URUGUAY | US VIRGIN ISLANDS | UZBEKISTAN | VAN

| BELGIUM | BELIZE | BERMUDA | BORA BORA | BRAZIL | BRITISH VIRGIN ISLANDS | BRITISH WEST INDIES | BRUNEI | BULGARIA | CAMBODIA | CANADA | CANARY ISLANDS |
GARCIA | DOMINICAN REPUBLIC | EGYPT | EL SALVADOR | ENGLAND | ERITREA | ETHIOPIA | FIJI | FRANCE | FRENCH POLYNESIA | GERMANY | GHANA | GIBRALTAR | GREECE |
| KAZAKHSTAN | KUWAIT | KWAJALEIN ISLAND | LEBANON | LIBYA | LITHUANIA | MACAU | MACEDONIA | MALAYSIA | MALDIVES | MALTA | MANCHURIA | MARSHALL ISLANDS
CALEDONIA | NEW GUINEA | NEW ZEALAND | NIGERIA | NORTHERN MARIANA ISLANDS | OMAN | PAKISTAN | PALAU | PANAMA | PERU | PHILIPPINES | POLAND | PORTUGAL |
H KOREA | SPAIN | SRI LANKA | ST. CROIX | ST. JOHN | ST. KITTS AND NEVIS | ST. LUCIA | ST. MARTIN | ST. THOMAS | ST. VINCENT AND THE GRENADINES | SWEDEN | SWITZERLAND
INE | UNITED ARAB EMIRATES | UNITED STATES OF AMERICA | URUGUAY | US VIRGIN ISLANDS | UZBEKISTAN | VANUATU | VENEZUELA | VIETNAM | WESTERN SAMOA | YEMEN

| BELGIUM | BELIZE | BERMUDA | BORA BORA | BRAZIL | BRITISH VIRGIN ISLANDS | BRITISH WEST INDIES | BRUNEI | BULGARIA | CAMBODIA | CANADA | CANARY ISLANDS |
GARCIA | DOMINICAN REPUBLIC | EGYPT | EL SALVADOR | ENGLAND | ERITREA | ETHIOPIA | FIJI | FRANCE | FRENCH POLYNESIA | GERMANY | GHANA | GIBRALTAR | GREECE |
| KAZAKHSTAN | KUWAIT | KWAJALEIN ISLAND | LEBANON | LIBYA | LITHUANIA | MACAU | MACEDONIA | MALAYSIA | MALDIVES | MALTA | MANCHURIA | MARSHALL ISLANDS
CALEDONIA | NEW GUINEA | NEW ZEALAND | NIGERIA | NORTHERN MARIANA ISLANDS | OMAN | PAKISTAN | PALAU | PANAMA | PERU | PHILIPPINES | POLAND | PORTUGAL |
H KOREA | SPAIN | SRI LANKA | ST. CROIX | ST. JOHN | ST. KITTS AND NEVIS | ST. LUCIA | ST. MARTIN | ST. THOMAS | ST. VINCENT AND THE GRENADINES | SWEDEN | SWITZERLAND
INE | UNITED ARAB EMIRATES | UNITED STATES OF AMERICA | URUGUAY | US VIRGIN ISLANDS | UZBEKISTAN | VANUATU | VENEZUELA | VIETNAM | WESTERN SAMOA | YEMEN

| BELGIUM | BELIZE | BERMUDA | BORA BORA | BRAZIL | BRITISH VIRGIN ISLANDS | BRITISH WEST INDIES | BRUNEI | BULGARIA | CAMBODIA | CANADA | CANARY ISLANDS |
GARCIA | DOMINICAN REPUBLIC | EGYPT | EL SALVADOR | ENGLAND | ERITREA | ETHIOPIA | FIJI | FRANCE | FRENCH POLYNESIA | GERMANY | GHANA | GIBRALTAR | GREECE |
| KAZAKHSTAN | KUWAIT | KWAJALEIN ISLAND | LEBANON | LIBYA | LITHUANIA | MACAU | MACEDONIA | MALAYSIA | MALDIVES | MALTA | MANCHURIA | MARSHALL ISLANDS
CALEDONIA | NEW GUINEA | NEW ZEALAND | NIGERIA | NORTHERN MARIANA ISLANDS | OMAN | PAKISTAN | PALAU | PANAMA | PERU | PHILIPPINES | POLAND | PORTUGAL |
H KOREA | SPAIN | SRI LANKA | ST. CROIX | ST. JOHN | ST. KITTS AND NEVIS | ST. LUCIA | ST. MARTIN | ST. THOMAS | ST. VINCENT AND THE GRENADINES | SWEDEN | SWITZERLAND
INE | UNITED ARAB EMIRATES | UNITED STATES OF AMERICA | URUGUAY | US VIRGIN ISLANDS | UZBEKISTAN | VANUATU | VENEZUELA | VIETNAM | WESTERN SAMOA | YEMEN

| BELGIUM | BELIZE | BERMUDA | BORA BORA | BRAZIL | BRITISH VIRGIN ISLANDS | BRITISH WEST INDIES | BRUNEI | BULGARIA | CAMBODIA | CANADA | CANARY ISLANDS |
GARCIA | DOMINICAN REPUBLIC | EGYPT | EL SALVADOR | ENGLAND | ERITREA | ETHIOPIA | FIJI | FRANCE | FRENCH POLYNESIA | GERMANY | GHANA | GIBRALTAR | GREECE |
| KAZAKHSTAN | KUWAIT | KWAJALEIN ISLAND | LEBANON | LIBYA | LITHUANIA | MACAU | MACEDONIA | MALAYSIA | MALDIVES | MALTA | MANCHURIA | MARSHALL ISLANDS
CALEDONIA | NEW GUINEA | NEW ZEALAND | NIGERIA | NORTHERN MARIANA ISLANDS | OMAN | PAKISTAN | PALAU | PANAMA | PERU | PHILIPPINES | POLAND | PORTUGAL |
H KOREA | SPAIN | SRI LANKA | ST. CROIX | ST. JOHN | ST. KITTS AND NEVIS | ST. LUCIA | ST. MARTIN | ST. THOMAS | ST. VINCENT AND THE GRENADINES | SWEDEN | SWITZERLAND
INE | UNITED ARAB EMIRATES | UNITED STATES OF AMERICA | URUGUAY | US VIRGIN ISLANDS | UZBEKISTAN | VANUATU | VENEZUELA | VIETNAM | WESTERN SAMOA | YEMEN

| BELGIUM | BELIZE | BERMUDA | BORA BORA | BRAZIL | BRITISH VIRGIN ISLANDS | BRITISH WEST INDIES | BRUNEI | BULGARIA | CAMBODIA | CANADA | CANARY ISLANDS |
GARCIA | DOMINICAN REPUBLIC | EGYPT | EL SALVADOR | ENGLAND | ERITREA | ETHIOPIA | FIJI | FRANCE | FRENCH POLYNESIA | GERMANY | GHANA | GIBRALTAR | GREECE |
| KAZAKHSTAN | KUWAIT | KWAJALEIN ISLAND | LEBANON | LIBYA | LITHUANIA | MACAU | MACEDONIA | MALAYSIA | MALDIVES | MALTA | MANCHURIA | MARSHALL ISLANDS
CALEDONIA | NEW GUINEA | NEW ZEALAND | NIGERIA | NORTHERN MARIANA ISLANDS | OMAN | PAKISTAN | PALAU | PANAMA | PERU | PHILIPPINES | POLAND | PORTUGAL |
H KOREA | SPAIN | SRI LANKA | ST. CROIX | ST. JOHN | ST. KITTS AND NEVIS | ST. LUCIA | ST. MARTIN | ST. THOMAS | ST. VINCENT AND THE GRENADINES | SWEDEN | SWITZERLAND
INE | UNITED ARAB EMIRATES | UNITED STATES OF AMERICA | URUGUAY | US VIRGIN ISLANDS | UZBEKISTAN | VANUATU | VENEZUELA | VIETNAM | WESTERN SAMOA | YEMEN

Trevor—

maybe the places here
are a little too "high end",
but their locations may be
worth exploring as you and Maddy
travel in the months and years
ahead.

Love,
Dad
Christmas '17

100 HOTELS + RESORTS

destinations that lift the spirit

images
Publishing

WATG

Published in Australia in 2012 by
The Images Publishing Group Pty Ltd
ABN 89 059 734 431
6 Bastow Place, Mulgrave, Victoria 3170, Australia
Tel: +61 3 9561 5544   Fax: +61 3 9561 4860
books@imagespublishing.com
www.imagespublishing.com

National Library of Australia Cataloguing-in-Publication entry:

Title:	100 hotels + resorts: destinations that lift the spirit / compiler, Wimberly Allison Tong & Goo.
ISBN:	978 1 86470 479 2 (hbk.)
Notes:	Includes index.
Subjects:	Hotels – Design.
	Resorts – Design.
	Resort architecture.
Also Titled:	One hundred hotels and resorts
Dewey Number:	728.5
WATG Editor:	Howard J. Wolff
IMAGES Coordinating Editor:	Andrew Hall
WATG Coordinating Editor:	Margaret Ann Michels
WATG Design Coordinator:	Jana Pesek
Production:	The Graphic Image Studio Pty Ltd, Mulgrave, Australia www.tgis.com.au
Printing:	Everbest Printing Co. Ltd., in Hong Kong/China

IMAGES has included on its website a page for special notices in relation to this and our other publications.
Please visit www.imagespublishing.com.

CONTENTS

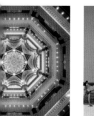     

PREFACE

by **the Senior Leaders of WATG**

We were honored to be asked by The Images Publishing Group to share the story behind the destinations designed by WATG. Honored and overwhelmed.

Beginning with the renovation of the Royal Hawaiian hotel in 1945, we made an early decision to specialize. Today, WATG has designed more hotels and resorts than any other firm on the planet, having worked on projects in 157 countries across six continents.

More than just a collection of pretty pictures, the 100 projects highlighted here were selected to reflect evolving trends in international travel and noteworthy preferences on the part of hotel guests and owners. They also illustrate how destinations can satisfy the distinct desires for rejuvenation, recreation, romance, excitement, escape, and enrichment.

Our projects take their inspiration from the qualities that make their locations unique. George 'Pete' Wimberly, the firm's founder, was creating architecture with a strong sense of place long before it was fashionable. And we're still heeding the principles of cultural authenticity and environmental sustainability.

The result, we hope, is a body of work that no longer renders the predictable acceptable. As different as WATG projects are from one another, our goal for each one is explicitly communicated in our firm's mission: to design experiences that lift the spirit.

Of course, none of our work would be possible without the vision and knowledge of clients who understand what people want and how to give it to them.

INTRODUCTION

by **Mary Scoviak**

For more than 60 years, the destination design firm WATG has not been following trends; it has been setting them.

Rejecting the idea that a hotel has to look functional to be functional, WATG has deconstructed the old notions about what made a hotel or resort popular and profitable. WATG stopped seeing architecture as a barrier and rethought it as a strategic interface between the world without and the world within. What WATG has taught guests, managers, and investors is that different is better, and that memorable is better still.

By infusing each of its projects with a sense of place, WATG's architects, planners, and designers create hotels and resorts that are experiences in themselves. The firm's talented staff draws on the best of local culture to immerse guests in an atmosphere that constantly reminds them of where they are and why they have come.

By marrying its own technical expertise and vast hotel experience with the wisdom of local builders, WATG has opened up new worlds for travelers—worlds as diverse as elegant, thatched-roof island resorts; white stuccoed retreats along the sea; chic casinos; meccas of urban entertainment; and palaces that blur created myth with sumptuous reality.

Exceeding guest expectations is an important element of successful design, but it is only one aspect. To be truly successful, a project must enhance the revenue opportunities for the manager and drive return on investment for the owner.

The combination of elegant, exciting aesthetics with a hard-working and efficient framework has a major impact on profit potential. Discerning travelers consistently rank WATG-designed hotels among the top in the world. Equally important, studies show that WATG's hotels and resorts typically maintain substantial rate premiums within their competitive set. Good architecture and design have driven up gross operating profits by double- and sometimes triple-digit figures following comprehensive renovation and repositioning. These are the palpable financial indicators of how successful WATG's approach has been and what a chord it has struck with the traveling public.

The measure of the success of WATG's visionary architecture and design lies in the long-lasting appeal of its hotels and resorts. Looking over the 100 projects featured in this book, it is difficult to assign an opening date to the properties. The designs are unique, timeless, and sustainable (in the broadest sense of the word), yet detailed enough to be "new" each time a guest returns.

WATG's projects expand our horizons and remind us that creativity has no limitations.

Mary Scoviak is editor of *Hospitality Style* and author of *International Hotel and Resort Design*. She was formerly design editor for *HOTELS* magazine and executive editor of *Hotels' Investment Outlook*.

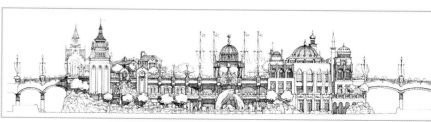

ANATOMY OF A DESTINATION

by **Michael S. Rubin, Ph.D.**

Today most of our leisure time is given over to amusements, to a hiatus from the work-a-day world. Yet the longing for the good life, for personal renewal, for enrichment and discovery, has never been greater. In an age in which every place is electronically accessible but remote from our touch, we seek remote places that offer access to new perspectives, discoveries, and encounters.

Creating a destination—a setting for leisure and renewal—is, therefore, a special kind of place-making. The destination is first and foremost an imagined place, an ideal experience we hope for in the future and cherish from the past. As an ideal place, the destination cannot simply be appreciated passively but requires participation in an experience that is, by definition, transitory. Physically and psychologically, the guest must leave a familiar world of routines to enter a novel realm of discovery and renewal. It is inevitable that the guest will eventually return to that world, but with the possibility that the place visited will provide a transformative experience.

For over six decades and across six continents, WATG has been on the leading edge of destination design. This is not simply because the firm has created more hotels and resorts than any other firm —quantity must take a back seat to quality in the architecture of destinations. Nor is it due to the fact that the firm has specialized in hospitality, leisure, and entertainment projects. It is that WATG has developed an architectural and interior design language that infuses destinations with a promise of transformation for their visitors.

Michael Rubin is president of MRA International, specializing in entertainment-based development.

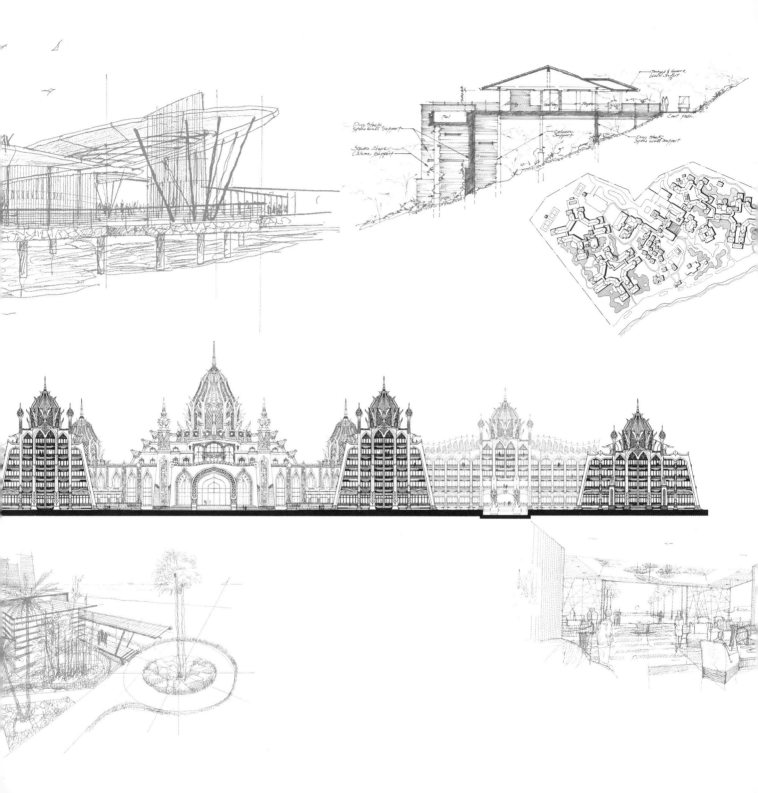

Drop Stacks
Stone Wall Support

Square Shape
Column Support

Tanooge & Garage
Wall Support

Cart Path

Pool

Column
Support

Drop Stacks
Stone Wall Support

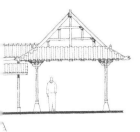

ASIA | PACIFIC

Tanjung Benoa, Bali, Indonesia

CONRAD BALI

Spectacular views out to the Indian Ocean and over the property's cascading pools greet guests in the open lobby lounge.

The hotel sits on acres of manicured gardens and lagoons that gracefully descend to the resort's wide expanse of beach and protected bay. Three guest wings in an E-shaped structure provide nearly all rooms and suites with ocean views. The entrance drive to the secluded property rises three levels to the porte-cochère, passing a waterfall flowing from the resort's lobby. Local materials and distinctive imagery were used to weave Balinese influences into every aspect of the guest experience.

A full-service conference center enables the resort to host international conferences and groups, while its ballroom facilities attract weddings and parties of all sizes. Guests can enjoy a wide variety of recreational options within this contemporary Balinese environment.

Rangali Island, Maldives

CONRAD MALDIVES RANGALI ISLAND

Accessed by a 30-minute seaplane flight from Malé, the resort is renowned for its idyllic setting on two private islands linked by a bridge and surrounded by a coral reef and lagoon.

Fifty of the resort's villas sit on stilts above a deep-blue lagoon in the Indian Ocean, with each villa featuring a glass-floored living room, a bedroom with a round, rotating bed, a bathroom, disappearing partitions and doors, and an outdoor balcony whirlpool. The spa rooms also offer mesmerizing views of marine life through their glass floors. Guests at the Spa Retreat stay in one of the luxurious Spa Water Villas that include stunning ocean views from all windows, a private treatment room, an outdoor bathtub, and a suspended sun deck.

The resort is also known for its attentive service, fine dining, and unique undersea restaurant. Miles of white-sand beach and unspoiled reef lure guests to partake of many water sports, including the diving for which the area is world-renowned. It's no surprise that such a heavenly place is host to many weddings and has been described as "the epitome of tropical paradise."

Bangkok, Thailand

FOUR SEASONS HOTEL BANGKOK

Modern in every respect, but also uniquely Thai, the hotel is designed as an elegant and efficient residence in the heart of a busy city.

STATS
353 guestrooms, including 18 suites and 8 guestroom cabanas; 4 restaurants and 3 lounges; 4.2-acre site

FEATURES
The Spa by MSpa, with full-service beauty salon; health club; ballroom, boardroom, function, and meeting rooms with state-of-the-art technology; business center; Executive Club; squash court; Bangkok's largest lap pool; private-entrance cabana rooms with poolside patios; retail arcade

KUDOS
Dream Hotels in Asia by *Esquire*
The Best Hotels in the World by *Travel+Leisure*
The Best City Hotel by Gallivanter's Awards

DON'T MISS
Taking the skytrain from right in front of the hotel—your gateway to the world of Bangkok

GUESTS SAY
"My first word would be WOW! This hotel is truly splendid! It's a wonderful sanctuary in the middle of Bangkok."

A traditional blue-tiled roof contrasts starkly with a gleaming white façade of plastered concrete, combining clean postmodern lines with classic Thai features. Artists and artisans worked with local materials such as hand-woven silks, teak, maka wood, and marble to give the hotel a distinctive feel.

Guestrooms open out onto two open-air atria which flank the main building core. Lush greenery spills down from each floor, along with waterfalls and lotus pools, recreating the feeling of the Thailand countryside right in the middle of Bangkok.

A carefully blended selection of traditional artwork, including an entire ceiling of hand-painted silk murals, makes the hotel's monumental lobby one of Bangkok's most acclaimed meeting places.

Tokyo, Japan

FOUR SEASONS HOTEL TOKYO AT CHINZAN-SO

A 17-acre park in metropolitan Tokyo provides the design focus for this hotel, specifically the park's historic and honored Japanese gardens, which are a favored setting for wedding ceremonies.

STATS
283 guestrooms, including 51 suites;
5 restaurants; 17-acre site

FEATURES
22,260-square-foot spa; fitness center; 26,000 square feet of banqueting and meeting space, including 16 conference rooms; 100-seat amphitheater; business center; indoor heated pool with retractable roof; shops and gallery; historic Japanese garden including an 800-year-old pagoda; Shinto shrine and chapel for wedding ceremonies

KUDOS
The Hot List by *Condé Nast Traveler*
Best Service in Asia by *Travel+Leisure*

DON'T MISS
Sampling the traditional Japanese *onsen* bath experience

GUESTS SAY
"I started my days here with a soak in the stone-crafted outdoor hot tub; with tree branches arching over it and located next to a waterfall, the tranquil setting creates the illusion that you are in the woods rather than in one of the world's largest cities."

In a marriage of Eastern and Western traditions, portions of the hotel's interior have a distinctly Japanese flavor, while the exterior is more contemporary with its angularity and huge expanses of glass. Suites are furnished in either a Western or Japanese style.

The hotel is designed to be a haven from stress in the middle of a frenetic city, so many public areas and guestrooms open onto the gardens. The conservatory-like spa features a luxurious *onsen* bath, with natural mineral water from the famous Ito hot springs, and a dramatic enclosed pool that has a barrel-vaulted roof to let in natural light and air.

Nusa Dua, Bali, Indonesia

GRAND HYATT BALI

This full-service luxury resort, located in the secluded and exclusive area of Nusa Dua, complements the terrain and culture of its beautiful and exotic island home.

Patterned after a Balinese village, the clay-roof buildings are organized into four decentralized clusters with their own courtyards and separate themes; all are connected by lighted, landscaped pathways to the main lobby village. In accordance with the local edict, no structure exceeds the height of a coconut tree.

The lobby/reception building derives its architectural character from the Balinese water palace, and waterfalls, pools, lagoons, and lotus ponds throughout the property reinforce this experience.

Larger structures spread among the landscaped grounds are designed to resemble Balinese ruins, while small shops are modeled after row houses.

Yalong Bay National Resort District, Sanya, Hainan, China

HILTON SANYA RESORT & SPA

Set amid 25 acres of coconut palms, lagoons, pools, sandy beaches, and terraces, the design of this resort draws inspiration from the rice terraces of central Hainan Island and incorporates local, natural materials.

Spacious guestrooms, suites, and villas are designed in a contemporary southern-Chinese style; the majority of accommodations overlook the crescent-shaped sandy beach and the South China Sea, while the remainder offer stunning views of the surrounding Yalong Bay National Park.

The array of restaurants and bars reflects the five traditional Chinese elements of metal, wood, water, fire, and earth, all in a contemporary fashion. The water-themed fine-dining restaurant features a floor-to-ceiling aquarium and glass floor over koi fish ponds.

Set apart from the main resort, the Spa Retreat comprises five single and three couple spa pavilions, a relaxation area, tea lounge, reflex zone, fitness center, and workout studio. Dedicated spa valets personally usher guests from their rooms to their spa pavilions, where they consult and tailor each rejuvenation program, including spa therapies, fitness regimes, health tips, and more.

Lantau Island, Hong Kong, China

HONG KONG DISNEYLAND® HOTEL

The flagship hotel of the Hong Kong Disneyland Resort® is a grand Victorian palace built on the shores of the South China Sea.

The hotel was designed to take the best advantage of two different views—one toward the activities of Hong Kong Harbour, the other overlooking the festivities of Hong Kong Disneyland®.

The design of the hotel draws from the most easily recognized stylistic patterns of Victorian architecture, including turrets, dormers, cupolas, exposed trusses, and band-sawed gingerbread. A grand salon features stained-glass domes, chandeliers, and potted palms, while a five-story lobby offers views through a large picture window to landscaped gardens and Penny's Bay beyond.

Spacious, well-appointed rooms and suites reflect the opulence and charm of the Victorian era. Designed to please guests with varying interests, the hotel has an array of amenities that include a spa, meeting facilities, a wedding gazebo, and a hedge maze in the shape of Mickey Mouse's head.

Coolum Beach, Queensland, Australia

HYATT REGENCY COOLUM

Situated on Australia's beautiful Sunshine Coast, at the base of Mount Coolum and amid lush rainforests, woodlands, and bush land, this popular destination was conceived as a health management resort village.

Hyatt Regency Coolum is unique in its decentralized, campus-like layout, which was designed to give the resort a residential feel and promote relaxation as well as stimulation.

The golf clubhouse doubles as the resort's reception building. Guest quarters are grouped in three low-rise clusters set amongst the trees. Nine lounge buildings that function much like clubhouses invite guests to gather for breakfast and a variety of informal social activities throughout the day.

The resort's architecture is inspired by elements of the Queensland style: lattices, trellises, and louvers provide shade and create interesting patterns and textures. Similarly, colors are borrowed from those seen in Coolum's nearby rainforests, mountains, coastal marshes, and beaches.

Hua Hin, Thailand

HYATT REGENCY HUA HIN

A much sought-after destination on the Gulf of Thailand with miles of white sandy beach, it's no wonder that Hua Hin has long been the summer resort choice for the Thai royal family.

STATS
204 guestrooms, including suites and villas; 4 restaurants and bars; 12.5-acre site

FEATURES
The Barai spa; Club Olympus fitness club; 6 function/meeting rooms and Grand Ballroom; business center; Regency Club; outdoor tennis courts; river pool and lagoon pool with water slide, beach pool, and children's pool; gift shop; Camp Hyatt

KUDOS
Best New Spa by TTG Travel Awards
Best Resort Spa by SpaAsia Crystal Awards

DON'T MISS
Exotic spa treatment rituals based on balancing the four elements: water, earth, air, and fire

GUESTS SAY
"The architecture and ambience exemplify total contemporary luxury; lovely rooms with fantastic bathrooms, beautiful gardens and pools, and plenty to do (or not)."

Designed as a contemporary interpretation of traditional Thai architecture, the resort was planned around the existing mature trees on the property. Guest accommodations are configured as low-rise clusters set among beautifully landscaped gardens and interconnecting pools. Large and airy with luxurious bathrooms, some guestrooms offer balconies, while ground-floor rooms include enclosed outdoor spaces. In all cases, the outdoor areas were designed as an extension of the living space. Similiarly, restaurants and bars are set in tropical gardens and around lagoons with spectacular views of the Gulf of Thailand.

The Regency Club is located in an exclusive wing of the hotel and features 61 rooms and suites. Amenities include a private swimming pool, garden, and lounge.

Active guests can enjoy a range of watersports as well as indoor and outdoor recreational activities for all ages. For those seeking pure relaxation, the spa offers exotic treatments in 18 rooms and eight suites designed to celebrate the Khmer style of art and blend the indoors and out.

Jeju Island, South Korea

HYATT REGENCY JEJU

Nestled within landscaped gardens on a panoramic cliff, the hotel overlooks Jungmun Beach on the East China Sea and offers 360-degree vistas of Jeju island.

STATS
224 guestrooms, including 18 suites and 1 presidential suite; 5 restaurants, bars and lounge; 10-acre site

FEATURES
Health club; conference/meeting/function space; business center; tennis courts; indoor–outdoor swimming pool; 9-hole putting green

KUDOS
Best Service Award by Hankook Ilbo
Best Hotel Award by PATA
Best Service Award by KNTO: Joongmoon Tourist Area

DON'T MISS
A visit to nearby Hallim Park, filled with a stunning variety of flowers, a Bonsai tree area, and two walk-through lava caves

GUESTS SAY
"The hotel lobby is particularly beautiful, with a koi fish pond and an expansive, open atrium with glass elevators."

The domed structures, which recall one of the predominant Korean cultural forms (the octagon), are also reminiscent of the island's indigenous architectural idiom: stone and thatched-roof village huts.

Forty of the guestrooms are Korean-style with *ondol* floors, which are heated by coals underneath the surface. Guests sleep in comfort on soft cushions, enjoying the gentle warmth of this radiant heat. Each of the hotel's 224 guestrooms and suites has its own private terrace with a view of either the gardens or the ocean.

INTERCONTINENTAL JAKARTA MIDPLAZA

Located in the heart of Jakarta's Central Business District, this luxurious urban hotel is perfectly situated for easy access to all businesses and shopping centers in the area.

STATS
321 guestrooms, including 77 suites;
2 restaurants and 3 bars/lounges; 3.5-acre site

FEATURES
Wellness center and spa; 24-hour fitness center;
18 multi-purpose meeting rooms, including
grand ballroom; 24-hour business center with
3 boardrooms; tennis court; swimming pool;
specialty retail arcade; children's playground;
gardens

KUDOS
Leading Hotel - Indonesia
by World Travel Awards

DON'T MISS
The hotel's large swimming pool in a beautiful
Balinese landscape garden, situated right in the
heart of Jakarta

GUESTS SAY
"The rooms in this first-rate hotel are quiet and
spacious with a sleek, modern design. There are
beautiful garden views to be found, even though
you are in the midst of a busy city."

The streamlined 11-story tower is clad in black marble with brown polished wood, creating a striking modern landmark. The hotel's unique entrance features a three-story-high lobby that serves as a gathering place for business and leisure travelers from around the world. In addition to hotel guests, the building houses 260 luxury condominium residences on the upper floors, most with views overlooking Jakarta's skyline.

Guests and residents can enjoy a variety of food and beverage venues within the hotel, or they can travel via an underground passageway to an adjacent building complex where there are 18 speciality restaurants. Relaxation in the hotel's spa can be found in any one of a number of treatments, ranging from reflexology and Shiatsu, to Thai and Indonesian massage.

Beijing, China

JW MARRIOTT HOTEL BEIJING

Located in the central business district of Beijing, this contemporary hotel is an integral part of China Central Place, a prestigious landmark of the capital city.

The 20-story JW Marriott Hotel Beijing anchors the Central Park and steps up from the River Walk experience created by the surrounding office and retail complex. Capitalizing on its location within a landscaped urban oasis, the majority of the guestrooms—as well as the spa, restaurants, and public areas—are oriented toward the park. In addition to the multi-level gardens, water features—both inside and outside—link the site's two hotels (the other being The Ritz-Carlton, Beijing) with the other components of this mixed-use development.

Both in form and in materials, the hotel's spaces manage to convey an atmosphere that is modern and sleek as well as warm and relaxing. Paying homage to China's thriving art scene, vibrant contemporary paintings adorn the hotel's walls, and the guestrooms feature the latest in-room technology. The glass, metal, and stone chosen by the architects for this property reflect a progressive aesthetic that is appropriate to today's Beijing and to the high-quality standards of a five-star experience.

Kuala Lumpur, Malaysia

MANDARIN ORIENTAL KUALA LUMPUR

Designed as an urban resort on the park, this 32-story hotel thrives in a competitive market by attracting visitors both from around the city and around the world.

STATS
643 guestrooms, suites, and executive apartments;
5 restaurants and 1 lounge; 2-acre site

FEATURES
The Spa at Mandarin Oriental Kuala Lumpur;
Vitality Club; fitness center;
15 meeting/function rooms; Grand Ballroom and
Diamond Ballroom; business center;
2 tennis courts; edgeless outdoor pool

KUDOS
World's Best Business Hotels
by Condé Nast Traveler
Best Hotels and Resorts by DestinAsian
Top 50 Hotels in Asia by Travel+Leisure

DON'T MISS
A unique outdoor swimming pool on the hotel's
fourth floor that appears to flow directly into the
50-acre park beyond

GUESTS SAY
"Everything about this hotel oozes quality, class,
and sophistication. We were so impressed,
we barely left the sanctuary of the hotel."

Located in the heart of the city, adjacent to the Petronas Twin Towers and fronting a 50-acre park, architects designed this hotel to uphold international standards and, at the same time, reflect traditional Malaysian influences. This was accomplished by using granite and wood from the region and by featuring Malaysian design details as well as local artworks and artifacts throughout. Curves in walls, in spaces, and in furnishings help to create a feeling of openness in the property, which extends to the luxurious and spacious guestrooms that offer spectacular city views.

The hotel's extensive conference and banqueting facilities, as well as its five distinctive restaurants, appeal both to visitors and residents of Kuala Lumpur.

Sawangan, Bali, Indonesia

NIKKO BALI RESORT & SPA

The hotel's design takes full advantage of its breathtaking placement on a natural bluff above a dramatic limestone cliff.

STATS
386 guestrooms and suites; 4 restaurants and 2 bars; 35-acre site

FEATURES
Mandara Spa; fitness center; Graha Sawangan Ballroom and meeting rooms; business center; marine sports; covered tennis center; 4 interconnected swimming pools, including a 98-foot water slide; Balinese water court; retail boutique; Jungle Camp; Wiwaha Chapel; amphitheater

KUDOS
Bronze Medal Award in Tri Hita Karana by *Bali Travel News*

DON'T MISS
The connecting pools, with water basketball and volleyball as well as a water slide

GUESTS SAY
"I tell myself that I should try out different hotels, but I find myself coming back time and time again because it is just fantastic in every way. The nikko is my Bali home. Period."

Balinese artwork and water courts throughout the property, along with materials such as coral stone and a touch of red Balinese brick, link the hotel with its location.

Cliff-side guestrooms provide dramatic views, as does the main lobby, which sits 46 feet above the turquoise waters of the Indian Ocean. Each of the luxurious spa villas is equipped with a private outdoor Balinese bath and garden shower.

A dramatic, 14-story (130-foot) cliff-hugging tower on the property offers a stunning outlook from the top. Upon descending, guests can find a secluded, private beach and stimulating esplanade that leads to the restaurants, spa, and authentic Balinese amphitheater.

Kuala Lumpur, Malaysia

PALACE OF THE GOLDEN HORSES

Situated on the shore of a picturesque 150-acre lake in MINES Resort City, this hotel is designed around a series of courtyards and sun-protected open spaces, in keeping with the tropical climate.

STATS
480 guestrooms including 80 suites; 5 restaurants and 2 lounges; 13-acre site

FEATURES
Jojobali Spa; fitness center and Palace Health Sanctuary; conference center with 2 ballrooms, 318-seat auditorium, and 21 meeting rooms; business center; landscaped pool; 18-hole golf course at MINES Resort & Golf Club; Golden Stable retail; MINES Wonderland and MINES Resort City

KUDOS
Gold Key Award by *Meetings & Conventions*
World's Hottest New Hotel by *Condé Nast Traveler*
Best New City Hotel in Asia Pacific by *Travel Trade Gazette Asia*

DON'T MISS
The shops at MINES Shopping Fair, where you can pick up a good bargain

GUESTS SAY
"A fine and spacious hotel with a beautiful pool."

The Palace of the Golden Horses is a contemporary reflection of the British Colonial-period design common to Malaysia. Blending the best of Moorish and Malaysian architecture, the hotel is characterized by a variety of towers and domes that provide multiple observation points overlooking the lake and surrounding hills.

Malaysian influence can be seen throughout the hotel in the use of traditional textiles, historic architectural features, and local flora and fauna. The swimming pool functions as an integral part of a botanical garden.

A Dignitaries Floor has its own business center, lounges, concierge, and butler service. The conference center is secluded in a private wing of the hotel and can seat up to 2,000 people. Activities that are part of the 1,000-acre MINES Resort City are linked to the hotel by water.

Singapore

PAN PACIFIC SINGAPORE

An extensive renovation program has established a new benchmark for excellence in luxury business accommodations located in the heart of the city.

STATS
775 guestrooms and suites; 6 restaurants and a lounge; 49.5-acre site

FEATURES
Spa; fitness center; 34,000 square feet of meeting space (24 venues); 8,661-square-foot ballroom; Executive Center level with a full-service, 24-hour business center, meeting rooms, and dedicated concierge; 2 tennis courts; indoor–outdoor recreational level; swimming pool with underwater acoustics; covered sky bridge to shopping mall

KUDOS
Asia's Leading Business Hotel by World Travel Awards

Top 50 Asian Hotels by *Condé Nast Traveler*

Top 10 Singapore Hotels by *Condé Nast Traveler*

DON'T MISS
The striking images of Singapore's national flower, the Miss Vanda Joachim Orchid, in a lobby mosaic of cut glass tiles imported from Italy

GUESTS SAY
"Full-length glass windows offer awesome views of Singapore's city skyline and Marina Bay Harbour."

The design of teak-louvered screen walls allows the opulent 35-story atrium lobby space to be divided into intimate seating areas. Housed within the innovative lobby structures, an intelligent lighting system is programmed to set the mood of the day or evening. The Executive Center—with a dedicated concierge, office staff, business club, meeting rooms, lounges, and boardrooms—attracts international clientele.

Guests can select accommodations from among 775 luxurious rooms and suites with privileges that range from around-the-clock butler service and use of board and meeting rooms, to secretarial services and all-day refreshments.

Shoufeng Township, Hualien, Taiwan

PROMISED LAND RESORT & LAGOON

Facing the Central and Shore mountain ranges, this captivating resort is centered among three islands, with bridges woven throughout lush gardens, lakes, and lagoons.

STATS
19 lagoon cottage buildings and 260 rooms with 66 suites; 2 restaurants, 1 bar; 37-acre site

FEATURES
Ayurveda Spa and hot spring; fitness center; 9,332 square feet of meeting space; business center; tennis courts; 3 outdoor swimming pools; 3 whirlpools; retail village; 1.4 miles of lagoon with water taxis; gardens; arcades

KUDOS
Best Hotel in Taiwan by China Post

DON'T MISS
Sipping a creative cocktail at the Chi-Lai Mountain House, where visitors feel as if they are inside a deep mountain cave enjoying performances by local musicians

GUESTS SAY
"There's a free boat ride round the resort for all guests. Overall, it's a great destination for both families and couples who just want to relax!"

Located on Taiwan's eastern coast, Promised Land is the country's first world-class resort. The hotel design combines the flair of Gaudi-style Spanish architecture, with its exquisite exterior design details, and the natural wonders of Hualien.

The hotel and cottages were designed so that every room overlooks the water and enjoys its own private lawn. A man-made lagoon, lake, lush gardens, and bridges are woven through the property.

The elegant and serene dining space of Aroma Restaurant integrates the aesthetics of Gothic architecture with the beauty of Chinese calligraphy in its design. The unique and beautifully designed ceiling is decorated with the poetry of famous Chinese calligraphers from different dynasties.

Tianjin, China

RENAISSANCE TIANJIN TEDA HOTEL & CONVENTION CENTRE

Conference delegates and business travelers flock to this property, known for its distinctive level of luxury and artful blend of Eastern and Western hospitality.

STATS
543 guestrooms, including 77 suites; 3 restaurants and 3 lounges/bars; 1.53-acre site

FEATURES
Health club; 66,736 square feet of meeting and exhibition space, including 18 meeting/function rooms, a 793-seat, 3-level auditorium, and 3 ballrooms; business center; 25-meter indoor swimming pool; shopping arcade; Renaissance garden

KUDOS
Best Convention Hotel in China (Top 10) by The 1st China (International) Convention Committee Conference
Best Business Hotel by M Media Group
Best Business Hotel in China by *Business Traveler*

DON'T MISS
The chance to savor the exquisite Cantonese cuisine in one of 12 private dining rooms at the hotel's Wan Li restaurant

GUESTS SAY
"An oasis in the middle of the Tianjin Economic Development Area with high-tech, stylish rooms."

Set in the heart of the prosperous Tianjin Economic and Technological Development Area (TEDA), the hotel has earned a reputation among conference delegates and business travelers from around the globe.

Architects designed an undulating glazed wall to complement the sweeping curve of an existing building. A colonnade ties the hotel tower to the conference center, where an illuminated and domed rotunda enlivens the gathering spaces. Guests can unwind in the health club or 25-meter pool and enjoy any one of the fine dining establishments on the property.

Hongqiao, Shanghai, China

SANDALWOOD PRIVATE RESORT

Neighboring a peaceful lake in the prestigious district of Hongqiao, an exclusive residential enclave of palatial homes offers 18 majestic estates designed for the lifestyle connoisseur with high expectations and worldly aspirations.

STATS
18 villas; 9.9-acre site

FEATURES
Jacuzzi, dry sauna, wet sauna; gymnasium; indoor swimming pool; solarium; libraries; formal dining rooms; private theaters; Western- and Chinese-style kitchens; classic landscaped gardens

KUDOS
No. 1 of China's Top Ten Super Villas by Washington News Agency

Top 50 Exceptional Model Houses by Urban Construction and Real Estate Scientific Development

Top 10 Villas of the Year by Chinese Elite Almanac

DON'T MISS
The unprecedented pampering of world-class butler services and the comfort of personal security experts

GUESTS SAY
"We had to pinch ourselves to ensure it was real."

Conceived and marketed as "private resorts," these residences draw their inspiration from the grandness and opulence of European tradition, while also maintaining their own distinctive identity.

The entrance to this gated community is defined by elegant wrought-iron gates set into a stone wall, embraced by manicured gardens and sparkling fountains. Each villa has its own decorative touches—such as frescoes, rare silk, and wood furnishings—and design elements—such as pillars, arches and wooden gates—that define the home's distinct architectural style.

All major rooms are oriented to the south to ensure that the villas have a light and airy feeling. Each offers both Western- and Chinese-style kitchens and a minimum of five bedrooms, including a luxurious master bedroom suite. Residents can entertain in the private screening room or relax in their grand solarium or private spa.

Singapore

SHANGRI-LA HOTEL, SINGAPORE, GARDEN WING

Set amid 15 acres of tropical gardens near the renowned Orchard Road shopping and business district, the Shangri-La Garden Wing reinforces Singapore's identity as Asia's Garden City.

The Shangri-La garden is home to more than 133,000 plants, flowers, and trees of more than 110 varieties—from ornamental flowering trees to aquatic plants, and from vibrant tropical flowers to shady fruit trees. It is also home to 200 Japanese koi, colored in luminous hues of red and gold, that reside in ponds filled by tumbling waterfalls.

The low-rise Garden Wing was designed as a separate and distinct sculpture from all sides. Its scale counterbalances the vertical high-rise Tower Wing and modern Valley Wing, yet the design imitates the curves of the original building. Lavishly infused with foliage, the Garden Wing's waterfalls, bridges, and paths provide a tranquil ambience that merges interior and exterior.

Comprising a three-story-high rock garden, the nine-story Garden Wing is famous for its spacious rooms and suites with bougainvillea-laden projected balconies. The Garden Wing is alive with the peaceful sights and sounds of the tropics and offers an oasis from the frenetic energy of a modern cosmopolitan city.

Nanjing, China

SOFITEL ZHONGSHAN GOLF RESORT NANJING

Located near the historical city of Nanjing, this European-style retreat overlooks the rolling hills of a Gary Player Signature golf course.

STATS
140 guestrooms, including 14 suites;
3 restaurants and 3 bar/lounges; 5.7-acre site

FEATURES
Day spa with massage facilities; fitness center;
conference facility with ballroom and 3 meeting
rooms; business center; tennis court; indoor
swimming pool and children's pool; 27-hole and
18-hole golf courses; retail; Mahjong room;
table tennis

DON'T MISS
A visit to nearby historic monuments,
tombs, and temples

GUESTS SAY
"The facilities, service, and dining exceeded my
expectations. I strongly recommend the resort as
a luxurious alternative to staying in the city."

The hotel and clubhouse, along with an international-quality conference center to host meetings for the national games, were designed to match the prestige of the golf course. The three main components of the resort were arranged to maximize views of a very picturesque site, with low hills to the back and a verdant golf course at the front.

A large and formally landscaped entry drive sets up a dramatic arrival experience, and the hotel's elegant lobby opens out to the golf course with views over a man-made lake that extends to a terrace overlooking the 18th green. The clubhouse is physically linked to the hotel by a sky-lit fitness and recreation facility. Arched colonnades and grand stairs add to the stately atmosphere, while quietly letting the natural beauty of the site shine through.

Non-golfers have plenty of leisure activities to choose from, and those whose purpose is business will find a full-service conference facility equipped with the most advanced technology.

Singapore

SWISSÔTEL MERCHANT COURT, SINGAPORE

Wide overhanging eaves and colonnades that open to landscaped gardens contribute to the tropical ambience of this urban resort.

STATS
476 guestrooms; 3 restaurants and bars;
2.3-acre site

FEATURES
Amrita Spa; 5 function rooms with conference
facilities; business center; pool deck with
free-form pool and poolside bars; retail

KUDOS
Tourism Hotel of the Year – Restaurant
by Singapore Tourism Board
Superstar Award by Singapore Hotel Association

DON'T MISS
Immediate access to all the action at Clarke Quay,
Boat Quay, and Chinatown

GUESTS SAY:
"A lovely hotel in an excellent location."

In keeping with the rich heritage and style of architecture in the area, pitched roofs with traditional unglazed tiles were used on the 12-story main structure and two five-story arms. The materials used for the structure—such as concrete with white stucco and brick trim—reflect those used on traditional shop houses in the city.

Within walking distance of Singapore's financial hub and near a central shopping mall and transport station, the Swissôtel Merchant Court offers the best of both worlds for those traveling for business or pleasure. Opposite the hotel is a bounty of dining and entertainment hot spots; inside, guests can enjoy the more tranquil feeling of a resort.

On the property, guests can choose from a selection of unique restaurants and bars, lounge on the landscaped pool deck, and indulge in spa facilities offering a full range of therapeutic treatments. Function rooms and a column-free ballroom host many of Singapore's banquets, seminars, and conferences. Three floors are dedicated to business travelers as part of an Executive Club.

Kuala, Terengganu, Malaysia

TANJONG JARA RESORT

Awarded the prestigious Aga Khan Award for its architecture, this sanctuary of luxury and well-being is steeped in age-old Malay traditions.

STATS
99 guestrooms; 3 restaurants; 42-acre site

FEATURES
Spa Village; fitness center; conference hall; tennis and squash courts; 2 swimming pools; water sports center; gift shop; library

KUDOS
Aga Khan Award for Architecture

Five Star Diamond Award by The American Academy of Hospitality Sciences

One of the Seven Natural Wonders of the World by *Condé Nast Traveler*

DON'T MISS
An outdoor Malay floral bath with candles, romantic music, and fragrances

GUESTS SAY
"Tanjong Jara is the sort of place that allows you to just step off from the world for a while. We have never relaxed so completely on holiday before."

The basic design motif for Tanjong Jara stems from the elegantly crafted wooden palaces (*istanas*) of Malaysian sultans. Native craftspeople relearned traditional building skills to construct the resort almost exclusively of native timber that is abundant in the area. None of the original buildings is higher than a coconut tree and the rooftops are made of local bisque tile.

Throughout the property, guests find authentic Malaysian arts and crafts and an opportunity to experience the local culture in myriad ways—from taking regional cooking lessons, to diving and snorkeling off of a private island, to indulging in a spa treatment that incorporates traditional healing methods.

Recently renovated to deluxe international standards, the resort's original beauty and Malaysian feel have been successfully preserved.

Mobor, Goa, India

THE LEELA KEMPINSKI GOA

Designed in a style that is reminiscent of the palaces of southern India, this resort is set amid lush gardens and lagoons, overlooking the Indian Ocean.

Designed to reflect Goa's unique culture and geographical location, The Leela combines South India's temple traditions with its Portuguese heritage. The main entrance features natural stone corbels with engraved motifs, while bronze idols and stone-carved sculptures of mythological animals adorn the hotel's public spaces.

All of the guestrooms are spacious, and each has a soothing, natural view over one of the property's sparkling lagoons. Marble bathrooms lend opulence, and carefully selected objets d'art create both an ancient Indian and Goan aesthetic. All accommodations include a private terrace, and some suites feature private plunge pools.

Whether relaxing under intricately carved friezes in the open-air pink sandstone lobby, or indulging in a regionally inspired treatment at the resort's spa, guests at The Leela enjoy the melding of India's cultural heritage with world-class standards for luxury.

Bangalore, India

THE LEELA PALACE KEMPINSKI, BANGALORE

Though close to the city's airports and urban business district, this luxurious hotel sits in an island of greenery, amid acres of lushly landscaped gardens and an azure lagoon.

Harking back to the royal heritage of the Vijaynagar Dynasty and the kingdom of Mysore, The Leela Palace features gold-leaf domes, ornate ceilings, and grand arches befitting its inspiration. Designed for the height of luxury and technology, the hotel marries the traditional past of Bangalore with its high tech present.

Guests can choose from over 300 opulent guestrooms and suites, including one in The Royal Club—a luxury hotel within a luxury hotel—with its own restaurant, bars, and lounges. Business travelers enjoy leading-edge technology in the hotel's conference facilities, and a full-service Ayurvedic spa and gymnasium are available to those looking for relaxation and recreation. The adjacent Leela Galleria features luxury boutiques, a beauty salon, and a sports center.

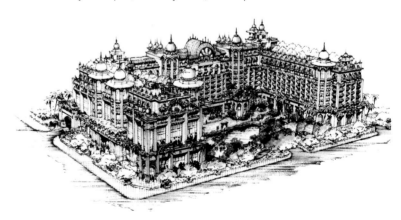

Bali, Indonesia

THE RITZ-CARLTON, BALI RESORT & SPA

The property perches dramatically on a bluff overlooking the Indian Ocean and offers guests the privacy of secluded, white-sand beaches.

STATS
368 guestrooms, including 38 new cliff villas; 12 restaurants and lounges; 173-acre site

FEATURES
Bali Thalasso & Spa with Aquatonic Seawater Therapy Pool, hydrotherapy treatment rooms, spa pavilion on a rock island, Japanese bathing room and gymnasium; 6,400-square-foot ballroom and 13,000 square feet of meeting space; business center; 3 tennis courts; two-tiered, fresh water swimming pool, 11,000-gallon outdoor saltwater aquarium and children's pool with water slide; 18-hole putting course; open-air dinner theater; 'Hidden Bali' culture tours

KUDOS
Top Five Asian Resorts by *Condé Nast Traveler*
Best Resort Spas Abroad by *Travel+Leisure*

DON'T MISS
On-site dining experiences that range from a five-course meal served on a private jetty, to the Dava restaurant in the shape of a lotus flower, to the Kisik bar and grill built into the cliffs

GUESTS SAY
"This resort is absolutely amazing: the attention to detail is unparalleled, the landscaping is a masterpiece, and the villas are the most beautiful and luxurious imaginable."

Bali's traditional architecture and natural beauty abound in the resort's 173 acres of lily ponds, sculptured fountains, and tiered lawns reminiscent of terraced rice paddies.

Guests can choose between accommodations in the four-story central building or one of the villas on site, including the large and luxurious "six-star" Bali Cliff Villas. The original *alang-alang* thatched roof villas offer ocean-view plunge pools with infinity edges, and each includes a *bale bengong*—a traditional open-air lounging area facing a peaceful garden courtyard.

The hotel's sensitivity to Balinese design can be seen in the low-rise massing and in details such as thatched roofing, brightly colored doors, limestone carvings, intricately woven mats, slate and marble floors, and limestone fences. In the lobby area, the ceiling is covered with Kamasan-style paintings, carefully lighted to emphasize the golden surface and accentuate the natural and cultural beauty of the island. Guests can visit the resort's award-winning spa, or stay at one of two "spa on the rocks" suites built atop huge rocks, accessed by wooden walkways.

Yalong Bay National Resort District, Sanya, Hainan, China

THE RITZ-CARLTON, SANYA

China's finest tropical seaside luxury resort combines contemporary and elegant architecture with a wide range of accommodations and dining experiences, designer-brand shopping, and a world-class spa on a secluded beach along the South China Sea.

STATS
450 guestrooms, including 33 pool villas and 21 suites; 8 restaurants and lounges; 37-acre site

FEATURES
ESPA including 24 treatment rooms and 6 spa suites; fitness center; 18,300 square feet of meeting space, including a ballroom and 9 meeting rooms; business center; 2 tennis courts; 4 swimming pools; boutique shopping arcade; on-site florist; wedding chapel; Ritz Kids®

KUDOS
Asia's Leading New Hotel by World Travel Awards

DONT MISS
Observing one of eight show kitchens and sampling menus that range from Cantonese to Italian to seafood and barbeque

GUESTS SAY
"Among all of the hotels on Hainan Island, this is one of the best by far; it's a great blend of contemporary design with Chinese sensibilities."

With its high, pitched ceilings; rich, dark woods; intricate carvings; and mosaic detailing—coupled with grand water features and opulent furnishings—the resort's design draws inspiration from Beijing's Summer Palace. Nestled between the pristine white-sand beach of Yalong Bay on one side and a mangrove reserve on the other, the property offers breathtaking views from all guestrooms.

Each of the villas includes a large deck with its own intimate infinity pool. The hotel's Lagoon guestrooms have a private Jacuzzi and are steps away from one of the resort's four swimming pools. Guests staying in the Club wing have personalized concierge services and a dedicated lounge. The effort to merge Asian graciousness with Western expectations can be seen not only in the resort's overall architectural design but also in its dining experiences, cultural activities, and spa treatment options.

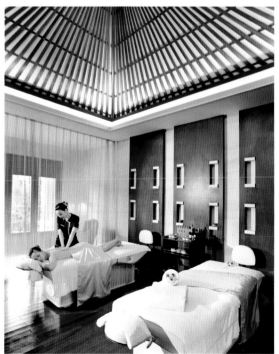

THE SHILLA JEJU

Behind the Mediterranean-inspired architecture—with its stucco walls, arched windows and portals, and terra-cotta tile roofs—is a hotel that easily accommodates Korean customs and lifestyles.

STATS
429 guestrooms, including 28 suites; 6 restaurants and bars; 21-acre site

FEATURES
Full-service spa; fitness club; 8 banquet halls; business center; tennis courts; indoor–outdoor pool; indoor golf range; duty-free shop; casino; arcade; kids' club

DON'T MISS
Walking through the grand gardens and down the staircase to the beach

GUESTS SAY
"The Shilla is amazing; the rooms are beyond luxurious and the gardens are magnificent."

Set in its own private 21-acre cliff-top gardens overlooking the Pacific Ocean, The Shilla Jeju is Korea's first luxury 5-star resort and has played host to numerous international conferences and high-level summits, impressing countless dignitaries from around the world.

While public spaces and function areas are designed to comfortably hold regal events, more intimately scaled spaces are created with design elements such as the glass-screen-tile-block dividing walls used in the lobby. Arriving guests enter a central building that presides over ocean vistas and radiates to four guest wings, each with uninterrupted views of the Pacific Ocean or Jungmun golf course and Mount Halla.

Singapore

THE ST. REGIS SINGAPORE

The first St. Regis hotel in Southeast Asia sets a new standard for hospitality in the region and serves as an emblem of Singapore's prominence as a 21st-century destination.

STATS
299 guestrooms and 173 residences; 3 restaurants and 3 lounges; 4.13-acre site

FEATURES
Remède® Spa; fitness center; 16,145 square feet of meeting space, including 6 function rooms and a ballroom; 24-hour business center; air-conditioned tennis court; outdoor pool; gift shop

KUDOS
Hot List Hotels by *Condé Nast Traveler*
T+L Editors' Choice Award by *Travel+Leisure*

DON'T MISS
The fleet of shiny Bentleys available to guests for chauffeured transportation

GUESTS SAY
"This hotel is absolutely amazing; the rooms are incredible and the dining is splendid."

Located in the heart of the city's premier shopping and business thoroughfare on Orchard Road, The St. Regis Singapore feels both vibrant and tranquil. From the sculpted lobby to the luxurious guestrooms and suites, the hotel's artistic heritage is apparent. In fact, The St. Regis houses one of the finest private art collections in Asia.

The distinctive, 20-story hotel is adjoined by two 23-story towers that provide 173 apartments, suites, and penthouses. Architects linked the three buildings by incorporating the crescent symbol of the nation's flag into the design. These crescent-shaped forms and profiles, clad in translucent glass, achieve a luminescent glow from the exterior.

An exclusive spa, fitness center, and beautiful outdoor pool are available to guests, as are the grand ballroom with skylights, several fine dining options, and the personalized services of a St. Regis butler. The St. Regis Singapore has already become a landmark for visitors and residents alike, impressing guests with its contemporary style of opulence.

EUROPE

London, United Kingdom

47 PARK STREET MARRIOTT GRAND RESIDENCE

Located minutes from Hyde Park and Bond Street, 47 Park Street offers its members the service and luxury of a five-star hotel and the comforts of their own homes, right in the heart of London.

Designing Europe's first urban fractional ownership property involved a complete architectural and interior modernization of the acclaimed Mayfair hotel, imbuing it with the atmosphere of an Edwardian-style townhouse and the amenities of a five-star vacation residence.

Each of the one- and two-bedroom residences was re-designed in a neo-Classical and Regency style; gold, cream, red, and blue furnishings help to create a refined and elegant atmosphere that feels distinctly British. The comfort and luxury of the residences come from the artful selection of finishes, which include Portuguese counter tiles and granite worktops in the kitchens, crystal light fixtures and Bouillotte desk lamps in the living rooms, mahogany head boards and fine Belgian linens in the bedrooms, and marble bathrooms adorned with period-style nickel fittings and faucets.

Crete, Greece

AMIRANDES GRECOTEL EXCLUSIVE RESORT

Water is an integral design element in this dazzling seaside resort on the north coast of Crete.

Amirandes Grecotel features an azure lagoon that sweeps around natural stone terraces, some with sunken seats for stunning views of the Cretan Sea and the setting sun. Stone arches and an uplifting atmosphere underscore the resort's luxury and refinement, and all of its amenities—including dining, spa, and conference hall—are back-dropped by views over the illuminated lagoon, the fine beach, and the glorious sea.

There is a range of accommodations across this landscaped property, from beautifully appointed guestrooms in the main building to family rooms with shared pools and bungalow suites arranged in the style of a traditional Mediterranean village. Designed like diminutive Creto–Venetian villas, these suites open to palm-studded, stone-laid decks with private pools set along the beachfront. Pergolas and sunbeds accent the feeling of leisure and luxury that permeates this unique water palace, a nod to the nearby archaeological site at the Palace of Knossos.

Aphrodite Hills, Cyprus

APHRODITE HILLS

The resort, now a premier destination on the west coast of Cyprus, is situated on a promontory nearby archaeological sites from the Greek, Roman, and early Christian eras, as well as the legendary Aphrodite's Rock.

The first integrated resort community in Cyprus, Aphrodite Hills was designed to include an international five-star hotel, a golf course with a clubhouse and golf inn, luxury villas, a retail center, tennis academy, health spa, tourist village, and a residential component. The retail center is the principal activity node, with shopping, dining, and entertainment options linked to a nearby amphitheater.

The InterContinental Hotel, at the heart of the property, was conceived as a retail village with guestroom clusters that cascade down the site to create a hillside town experience. With the elegance and ambience of a country manor home and the warmth of a stone farmhouse, the hotel becomes part of the topography.

Each of the resort's components has a distinctive architectural character, and all evoke the traditional village architecture of Cyprus.

London, England

CLARIDGE'S

For this major renovation and refurbishment of one of London's most prestigious hotels, immense care was taken to ensure that its style was preserved.

STATS
203 guestrooms, including 67 suites and
2 penthouse apartments; 1 restaurant and
4 lounges/bars; 1 city block site

FEATURES
Fitness and beauty suite; 9 banquet/meeting
rooms; retail shop

KUDOS
Top 100 Hotels in the World
by *Condé Nast Traveler*
Top 20 Foreign City Hotels
by Andrew Harper's *Hideaway Report*
Best Hotels in Europe by *Travel+Leisure*

DON'T MISS
Afternoon tea service of scones, double
Devonshire cream, and strawberry jams,
accompanied by a piano and violin duo

GUESTS SAY
"This is one of the world's finest hotels. Staying
here, you know you are in London."

The goal was to equip Claridge's with state-of-the-art, 21st-century conveniences while preserving the charm and detailing of this 100-year-old Grade II historic landmark—all while keeping its doors open. Restoration of period details was accomplished with the support of English Heritage, and an electronic record was created of the building and its contents.

All of the luxurious rooms have different layouts, furnishings, and finishes. A complete remodeling of the hotel's sixth and seventh floors (previously maids' chambers) provided two penthouse suites, deluxe double rooms, a conference suite of private meeting and banqueting rooms, and a health fitness suite. As part of the refurbishment, the latest in-room communications technology was discreetly installed.

DENIA MARRIOTT LA SELLA GOLF RESORT & SPA

This hotel has a relaxing, country estate feel and is designed to maximize the beautiful views it has over the La Sella golf course, towards the mountains and across Montgo National Park.

STATS
178 guestrooms, including 8 suites; 2 restaurants and 3 bars; 215,000-square-foot site

FEATURES
La Sella Spa; fitness facility; 6,700 square feet of meeting space including grand ballroom and breakout rooms; outdoor pool and whirlpool; 18-hole La Sella golf course

DON'T MISS
Activities from cooking classes to flamenco dancing, from horseback riding and wine tasting to regattas, beach sports, and tours of ancient landmarks

GUESTS SAY
"The hotel, situated in a lovely part of Spain, is fantastic. Our room was stunning—overlooking the mountains, swimming pool, and golf course."

Discrete courtyards and terraces give this resort a vernacular Spanish feel, which can also be felt in the cafés and restaurants. The hotel's entrance leads directly to a grand staircase and to the poolside with views over the verdant golf course—the first ever designed by José Maria Olazabal.

The resort's main courtyard is positioned to optimize views, as are the spacious guestrooms, each with a balcony. A grand ballroom for 400–500 guests and a full-service spa both link to the pool, and the main restaurant is overlooked by an elevated terrace. The resort's specialty restaurant is stylistically reminiscent of a *bodega* with classic Spanish bench seating.

Whatever one's tastes, and whatever the purpose of one's visit—business or pleasure—guests can choose from a wide range of options and activities.

Marne-La-Vallée, France

DISNEYLAND® HOTEL AT THE DISNEYLAND® RESORT PARIS

Designed as an elegant, turn-of-the-century Queen Anne Victorian styling mansion, the pastel-pink hotel—with its gingerbread styling, cupolas, chimneys, finials, and red-shingled roof—provides an enchanting fairytale ambience.

STATS
496 guestrooms including 18 suites;
2 restaurants and 1 lounge; 15.5-acre site

FEATURES
Fitness club; meeting rooms; indoor swimming
pool and pool house; retail shops;
arcade/game room

KUDOS
European Hotel of the Year
by the British Travel Agents Association

DON'T MISS
The utter convenience of being able to buy
Disneyland® tickets at the front desk and catching
a pink bus outside the front door for a five-minute
ride to the theme park

GUESTS SAY
"The room is great, the bed is great, the hotel's
atmosphere is great ... a wonderful experience
for kids and just as good for adults!"

As the destination's flagship resort, this hotel incorporates the entry gates to the Disneyland® Park in its design. Guests approach through Fantasia Gardens and enter a splendid lobby adorned with Cinderella's Fairytale Chandelier and a majestic sweeping staircase.

Many of the hotel's guestrooms overlook the Disneyland® Park or Fantasia Gardens, and top-floor suites have outstanding views of Sleeping Beauty Castle. The spacious guestrooms are decorated in pastel shades and incorporate Disney images throughout, such as on the tiled frieze in suite bathrooms.

All suites are individually themed, for example, the Cinderella Suite. Those on the hotel's top two floors have special amenities—a private elevator, separate reception desk, and lounge—that distinguish this 50-room boutique hotel within a hotel called the Castle Club.

Dublin, Ireland

FOUR SEASONS HOTEL DUBLIN

The hotel's windows open to the brilliant greenery and charming streetscapes of ivy-covered residences and embassies in Ballsbridge— the showgrounds of the historic Royal Dublin Society.

STATS
197 guestrooms, including 40 suites and 25 private residences; 3 restaurants and 3 lounges/bars; 3.5-acre site

FEATURES
Full-service spa; state-of-the-art fitness center; 15,000 square feet of meeting and function space; 24-hour business center; pool; Weir's Store; historic grounds and outdoor garden courtyard

KUDOS
Gallivanter Award for Excellence by Editor's Choice Awards
Gold List by *Condé Nast Traveler*
World's Best Hotel by City by Institutional Investor

DON'T MISS
VIP check-in for children or afternoon tea in The Living Room

GUESTS SAY
"The rooms were perfect, the service was extraordinary, and the atmosphere was incredible."

Despite its impressive size, this truly luxurious property manages to retain an atmosphere of comfort and intimacy. The red-brick hotel was designed to reflect Dublin's Georgian and Victorian character with updated accents to meet the contemporary tastes of today's international traveler. Spacious guestrooms and suites are elegantly designed in soft shades of color, each with a large marble bathroom.

With its high conservatory, The Seasons Restaurant is a beautiful setting for meals at any time of the day. Guests plan their days over coffee in the sunny Lobby Lounge, while contemporary art sets a dynamic and dramatic mood for evening drinks in the Ice Lounge.

GRECOTEL CAPE SOUNIO

The resort blends in with the landscape and sits on the edge of a national park next to one of the world's most celebrated archaeological sites.

STATS
149 bungalows, suites, and villas; 3 restaurants and 4 lounges/bars; 75-acre site

FEATURES
Elixir Spa '007; fitness club with cardio fitness room; 8,600 square feet of meeting space and 6 break-out rooms; outdoor terraces for special events; business center; 2 tennis courts; indoor and outdoor seawater pools with whirlpool and children's pool; nearby 18-hole Glyfda Golf Course; retail boutiques

KUDOS
Preferred Standards of Excellence by Preferred Hotels & Resorts Worldwide

DON'T MISS
Walking through colonnades and terraces, while catching vistas of archeological ruins

GUESTS SAY
"Relaxing in this magnificent setting delighted our senses. The design and the décor lifted our spirits and rejuvenated our souls."

Set against views of the Temple of Poseidon, the architecture honors the classical Greek tradition with elements such as colonnades and water features made from Greek marble. Natural stone and local timber, along with soft earth tones inside, help to integrate the resort into the natural landscape of the surrounding acropolis.

A glass boardwalk leads guests over the site's archeological ruins and a mirror pool at the center of the landscape reflects views of the nearby temple. While completely contemporary in its luxury, this resort never loses sight of the history and nature of the locale.

Corfu, Greece

GRECOTEL EVA PALACE

Kommeno peninsula, one of the most romantic spots in the Ionian Sea, harbors this intimate, exclusive hideaway designed for couples.

The main building, inspired by classical architecture, offers views of the stunning coastal villages and small islands that dot the Ionian Sea between Corfu and the mainland. Pastel-colored bungalows and villas with private pools sit amid lush olive trees and tranquil flower gardens.

Guests can stroll along winding pathways and either find solitude or enjoy the resort's stunning oasis pool. There, a floating grid of palms forms a living backdrop to a poolside bar, and floating pool decks become "evening dining islands." Other options for dining include terraces that cascade over wooded coves and offer spectacular ocean views.

Kos Island, Greece

GRECOTEL
KOS IMPERIAL THALASSO

On a hillside overlooking the sparkling Aegean, a series of free-form pools envelop this imperial playground.

STATS
384 guestrooms, including bungalows, suites, and villas; 4 restaurants and 2 lounges/bars; 24.7-acre site

FEATURES
Elixir Thalasso Spa; fitness room; Hippocrates Conference Hall; meeting rooms and outdoor terrace for functions; 5 pools (3 outdoor, 2 indoor); holiday boutiques; Grecoland Club

KUDOS
Platinum Collection "Best in Europe" by Thomson

DON'T MISS
The AquaElixir hydrotonic pool, uniquely decorated in aquamarine shades with Murano crystals and golden leaves, which offers all the regenerating effects of thalassotherapy

GUESTS SAY
"This lovely hotel is large but very cleverly laid out with plenty of beautiful gardens and pool areas."

Kos Imperial lies on the north coast of the island Kos, where the Greek seas merge with the seas of Turkey. The resort was designed as a water palace, with the main building and bungalows set amid pools, lagoons, and lush gardens. The landscape itself is part of the experience—island gardens cascade to the beach edge, a river swirls around a tiny island in the pool, and broad terraces are framed with drop-edge reflecting pools.

Guests can choose from a selection of villas, beachfront suites, bungalows, and penthouse suites. All are ultra-spacious and offer sweeping sea views. Dining options include a floating restaurant set on the lagoon.

Peloponnese, Greece

GRECOTEL OLYMPIA RIVIERA RESORT

Set on a 500-acre estate along a one-mile stretch of Greece's most beautiful coast is a luxurious retreat composed of five distinct environments.

Inspired by ancient Greek cities, the resort features low-rise buildings with clay tile roofs and consists of two luxury hotels, a thalassotherapy spa, and a state-of-the-art convention center. Inside the main buildings, marble pillars, friezes, cornices, and high ceilings suggest a modern interpretation of classic Greek and Mediterranean styles.

The Thalasso Hotel, centered around an elegant, three-tiered fresh water pool with views across Kyllini Bay, offers a luxurious spa experience. Families who choose the Oasis Hotel can enjoy water slides, lazy rivers, and beautifully landscaped tiered gardens. With so many different options—including numerous dining possibilities as well as an entertainment center with an amphitheater and six swimming pools—the resort delights all kinds of guests.

Cartagena, Murcia, Spain

HYATT REGENCY LA MANGA

Nestled between the low hills of the Murcian Mountains that separate the Mediterranean from the Mar Menor Sea, this luxury golf resort and hotel is host to a prominent spa.

STATS
189 guestrooms, including 6 luxury suites and one Royal Suite; residential apartments and villas; 11 restaurants and 8 lounge/bars; 1,400-acre site

FEATURES
Spa La Manga Club; 2 fitness centers; banquet, conference, and convention facilities; 28-court tennis center and tennis academy; 6-lane 25-meter indoor pool, separate kids' pool, and large open-air swimming pool; three 18-hole championship golf courses and golf academy; boutiques; soccer field; cricket field; crown green bowling

KUDOS
Leading Conference Hotel by World Travel Awards
Europe's Leading Golf Resort by World Travel Awards

DON'T MISS
Spa La Manga Club's offering of the *costa cálida*, including the cooling pure aloe body wrap and skin-softening olive oil marmalade application

GUESTS SAY
"Top choice for a completely relaxing resort-style break with a Spanish flavor."

Transforming a 1970s hotel into an Andalusian–Mediterranean-style five-star resort that remains true to the cultural and architectural heritage of southern Spain, the architects created a destination that manages to be at once both classic and contemporary.

State-of-the-art design elements are integrated with motifs found in historic Spanish villas of the early 18th century: arches, arcades, wrought iron railings, terra cotta roofs, and exposed terraces. The lobby's high vaulted ceiling, stone floor, and white walls suggest the entry hall of an old villa, with contemporary interpretations evident in the selection of fixtures and furnishings. The long, low wings of the Hyatt Regency La Manga settle into the surrounding terrain and mirror in style and scale the neighboring village architecture. The 1,400-acre sporting paradise is used as a training resort by professional golf, football, and tennis teams.

Limassol, Cyprus

LE MERIDIEN LIMASSOL SPA & RESORT

This luxurious "residents only" resort is renowned for its award-winning thalassotherapy spa, delicious array of dining options, dedicated children's facilities, and its range of spacious accommodations.

The resort's design takes its inspiration from the surrounding sea and the Cypriot lifestyle. The sea is used to greatest advantage, not just for its views from every room but also as a supplier of mineral salts, vitamins, and chlorophyll that are used in specialized spa therapies to promote relaxation and rejuvenation.

The luxurious seafront spa is completely immersed in orange, olive, and cypress trees, and local aromatic herbs are used as ground cover. This oasis of relaxation includes five outdoor seawater pools and three indoor pools—each with a different salinity content and temperature—as well as a steam bath, saunas, whirlpools, plunge pools, and 34 treatment rooms. Created as a "hotel within a hotel," the spa has its own accommodations.

Footpaths made of traditional Cyprus stone connect the various activities on the property, and spacious balconies accord stunning views of the sea, pool, gardens, and surrounding hills. While some suites and activities are designed to accommodate families, others are designed for adults only. Dining venues include Mediterranean, Italian, and Japanese options—many with menus just for kids.

Vilamoura, Algarve, Portugal

THE LAKE RESORT

With the endless Falésia beach on the horizon, the marina in the background, extensive gardens, and a private lake at your doorstep, this resort is an ideal setting to enjoy peaceful moments in pleasant company.

Neighboring an ecological reserve between the marina and the sea in the center of Vilamoura, the hotel and residential apartments blend seamlessly into the natural environment—they are surrounded by an artificial saltwater lake that creates a direct connection to the sea, permitting the renewal of natural water and encouraging development of maritime flora and fauna.

The design inspiration for this five-star resort hotel and luxury residential development comes from both the local Roman ruins and from the grand, traditional architecture of Portugal. The main lobby, covered by a 46-foot dome, has a neoclassical circular entrance, giant stone columns, and long, light curtains that wave gently in the wind.

Every room has a private balcony from which to enjoy panoramic views, and the resort's three outdoor pools include Europe's first sand-bottom swimming pool.

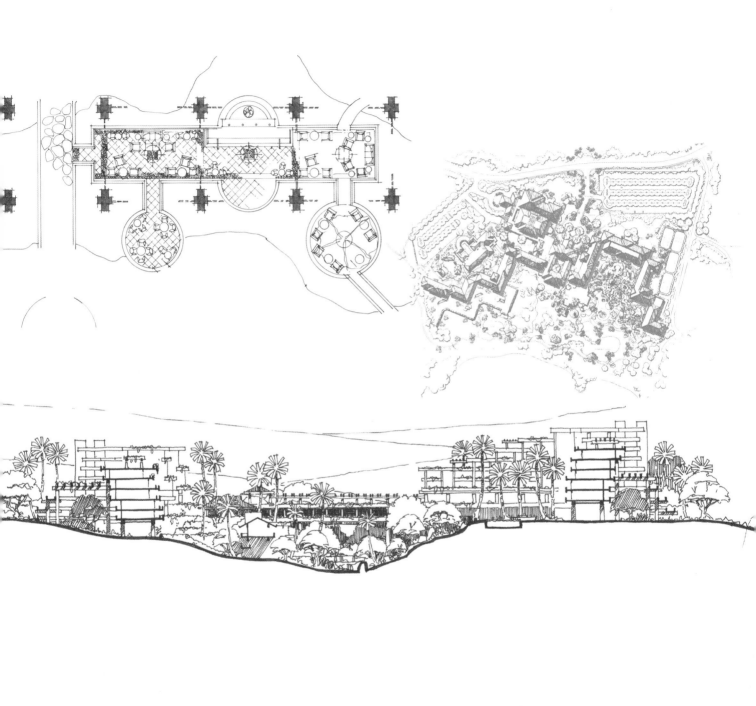

HAWAIIAN ISLANDS

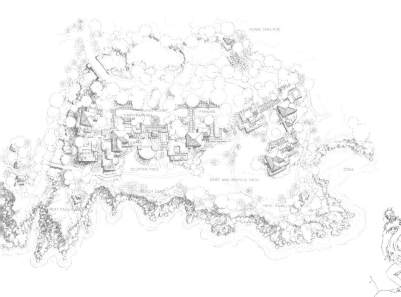

Wailea, Maui, Hawaii, USA

FOUR SEASONS RESORT MAUI AT WAILEA

Although palatial in style and proportion, the resort was designed to harmonize with its tropical setting and climate.

STATS
380 guestrooms, including 75 suites; 2 restaurants and a lounge; 15-acre site

FEATURES
Spa; fitness center; 24,000 square feet of meeting and function space; business center; tennis courts; 2 pools; 3 golf courses: Wailea Gold Course, Wailea Emerald Course, Wailea Blue Course; retail shops; library; Kids for All Seasons; water features and gardens

KUDOS
The World's Best Hotels by Travel+Leisure

DON'T MISS
Three golf courses that take full advantage of Wailea's naturally undulating terrain and stunning scenery, and challenge players with strategically placed bunkers and hazards as well as with changes in elevation

GUESTS SAY
"Absolute paradise; this is the perfect place. If you can't relax here, you can't relax anywhere."

Throughout the hotel, the architects have used a number of design elements to take advantage of—and enhance—the building's oceanfront setting, including cross ventilation; sun-protected and breeze-cooled open spaces; natural lighting; the blurring of boundaries between indoors and outdoors; the focus on water for sight, sound, and feel; and the use of lush, exotic plant materials. The U-shape of the building, the central courtyard facing the water, and guestrooms placed at a 45-degree angle to corridors provide 85 percent of the accommodations with an ocean view.

Guestrooms take their design inspiration from the four compass points of Maui: the mountains, ocean, volcano and sand. Their design features a blend of rich wood finishes for the furniture, *kapa*-inspired carpets, and an array of patterns and textures in the fixtures and furnishings that respond to the island's natural history and features.

GRAND HYATT KAUAI RESORT & SPA

Set on 50 oceanfront acres, the flow of open spaces throughout the resort keeps the atmosphere informal and appropriately reflective of Hawaii's climate and culture.

STATS
602 guestrooms; 6 restaurants and 5 lounges; 50-acre site

FEATURES
51,500-square-foot Anara Spa; fitness and health center; 65,000 square feet of banquet and meeting space; business center; 4 tennis courts; freshwater river pools with 150-foot water slide and 5-acre saltwater lagoon; 18-hole Robert Trent Jones II championship golf course; 12,000 square feet of retail space

KUDOS
The World's Best Hotels by *Travel+Leisure*
The World's Best Spas by *Travel+Leisure*
Top 100 Resorts Worldwide by *Condé Nast Traveler*

DON'T MISS
An outdoor *lomi lomi* massage, completely private thanks to curtains of plants and trees

GUESTS SAY
"Where the resort ends and the island begins is wonderfully ambiguous. It's like the architects wove the scenery into the lobby, restaurants, corridors, and guestrooms."

The resort stretches out amid lush gardens and lagoons, forming two wings of attached four-story buildings radiating from a central pavilion. Double-pitch roofs of green glazed tile mirror the green hues of nearby mountains and verdant countryside. Heat produced by the air conditioning system is used to warm the water for guestrooms, the laundry, and swimming pools in an effort to be environmentally sustainable.

A striking example of classic Hawaiian architecture of the 1920s and 30s, many of the resort's walls open to wide courtyards, gardens, and spectacular views. The resort's challenging oceanfront location inspired designers to incorporate the scenery while sheltering it from nature's wilder aspects, which include brisk trade winds, strong surf, and salt-laden air.

There is a timeless elegance in the hotel's detailing—including koa cabinetry and exposed wood beams as well as historical sugar cane and pineapple motifs throughout—that is evocative of Plantation-era design.

Kohala Coast, Big Island, Hawaii, USA

HAPUNA BEACH PRINCE HOTEL

When Laurance Rockefeller built the Mauna Kea Beach Hotel on a lava field overlooking a beautiful white sand beach, he envisioned a resort with two hotels and a golf course: The Hapuna Beach Prince Hotel completes that vision.

The hotel design took measures to protect the area's natural springs, which are the source of its name "Hapuna." Four low-rise structures overlook Hapuna Beach on two different levels and provide ocean views from the private deck of every guestroom and suite. Likewise, the hotel's large, open-air lobby was designed to be cooled naturally by Hawaii's gentle trade winds and to bring the spectacular views and nature inside. The use of multicolored slate in the resort's lush gardens of tropical plants and trees creates a sense of connectedness throughout the property.

Hapuna Golf Course has been nationally recognized for the challenging link-style course designed by Arnold Palmer and Ed Seay.

Honolulu, Oahu, Hawaii, USA

HAWAII CONVENTION CENTER

Sitting at the entrance to Waikiki, this gathering place combines the requirements of a state-of-the-art meetings facility with the beauty, comfort, and culture that are uniquely Hawaiian.

Nearly 63 percent of this award-winning convention center is open to the sky, taking advantage of the island's trade winds for natural ventilation. Other sustainable features include the 6 acres of landscaped grounds, terraces, and courtyards, as well as a 2.5-acre rooftop garden with flowing ponds and native flowers.

Inside, design features and artwork reflect the beauty of the tropical location and evoke images that are distinctly Hawaiian. A 70-foot misting waterfall plunges into the airy, glass-walled lobby, while a grand staircase and escalators offer panoramic views of the Ko'olau mountains in the distance. Soaring rooftop canopies recall images of Polynesian sailing canoes and also control solar gain.

A bronze statue fronting the Hawaii Convention Center symbolically acknowledges the Hawaiian people for their generosity and goodwill toward newcomers.

Waikiki Beach, Honolulu, Oahu, Hawaii, USA

HILTON HAWAIIAN VILLAGE BEACH RESORT & SPA

Waikiki's only true destination resort experience has evolved from a visionary master plan for a resort village.

Throughout the resort, space was planned to maximize the flow between indoors and out. The lobby's open-air reception pavilion overlooks a progression of water views: fountains, a 10,000-square-foot free-form swimming pool, and the Pacific Ocean. The varied hospitality functions—retail, convention, events, recreation, entertainment, and accommodation—are connected as part of a festive village, with tropical gardens, waterfalls, and exotic wildlife integrated throughout the property.

This self-contained destination, located on Waikiki's widest stretch of beach, is well known for its luxurious accommodations, wide assortment of leisure activities, and classic Hawaiian hospitality. Guests can enjoy much of what the islands offer without leaving the 22-acre village, from watersports and wildlife to Polynesian ceremonies and cuisine.

Kaanapali Beach, Lahaina, Maui, Hawaii, USA

HYATT REGENCY MAUI RESORT & SPA

The Hyatt Regency Maui Resort & Spa overlooks an intricate system of waterfalls, pools, and lagoons that meander and cascade through elaborate tropical and Japanese gardens.

STATS
806 guestrooms and suites; 6 restaurants including an on-site luau, 3 bar/lounges and a nightclub; 40-acre site

FEATURES
15,000-square-foot Spa Moana; 5,000-square-foot Moana Athletic Club; 125,000 square feet of indoor/outdoor function and exhibition space; business center; beach activity center; 6 championship tennis courts; 2 free-form swimming pools with waterfalls, tide pools, rope bridge, lava-tube slide, and swim-up underwater cave and Grotto Bar; Keiki Lagoon for kids; shuttles to 8 different 18-hole championship golf courses; retail shops; Camp Hyatt

KUDOS
Top 10 Hotels in Hawaii by *Celebrated Living*
Award of Excellence by *Corporate and Incentive Travel*
Gold Key Award by *Meetings and Conventions*

DON'T MISS
Viewing the stars through the "Great White" telescope—a unique cosmic experience

GUESTS SAY
"One can wander around the gardens for hours and find waterfalls, streams and small ponds, exotic animals, Asian art, and many secluded and peaceful places."

Occupying a 40-acre beachfront property on the Kaanapali Coast of Maui, the hotel's three mid-rise buildings incorporate native woods and regional artwork that reflect Hawaii's tropical environment and set a tone that is both elegant and informal. Extensive use of koa wood and hand-painted ceiling murals carry out the same theme in the hotel's ballroom, dining, and entertainment areas.

All rooms are designed with plantation-style wood furniture, cotton duvets, and Hawaiian quilt wall hangings, giving the rooms a residential feel. Each room also features a separate seating area and private lanai on which to enjoy panoramic views of the mountains or Pacific Ocean.

Waikiki, Oahu, Hawaii, USA

HYATT REGENCY WAIKIKI RESORT & SPA

At the center of the resort's twin towers is the Great Hall atrium, which features three-story waterfalls, exotic birds, and lush tropical foliage.

STATS
1,230 guestrooms, including 18 suites;
6 restaurants and 2 lounges; 2-acre site

FEATURES
Na Ho'ola Spa (2-story, 10,000 square feet);
fitness center; 29,000 square feet of function and
exhibit space; business center; outdoor swimming
pool and 2 whirlpools; 60 retail shops

KUDOS
Gold Key Award by *Meetings & Conventions*
Excellence Award by AIA Honolulu Chapter
Four Diamonds 23 consecutive years by AAA

DON'T MISS
Sitting on the wooden rocking chairs by
the pool or on the chaise lounges in the
spa, overlooking the surfers and waves
of Waikiki Beach

GUESTS SAY
"Above the fray of Waikiki is a beautiful hotel
with fantastic views."

The architects chose an octagonal configuration for the resort's two 40-story towers in order to maximize the views from the guestrooms. The open-air atrium, which connects the two towers, is encircled with retail shops that ascend all three levels and create a fun, tropical shopping ambience for guests. Na Ho'ola Spa (*Na ho'ola* means 'many healers') provides guests with a uniquely Hawaiian spa experience, both through its specialty treatments and its culturally inspired design. Adding to the sense of place, the spa overlooks Waikiki Beach and the Pacific Ocean.

Kapolei, Oahu, Hawaii, USA

MARRIOTT'S KO OLINA BEACH CLUB

This secluded beachfront oasis is nestled within Ko Olina Resort, a lush 642-acre gated community on the western shore of Oahu.

Design details throughout the beach club and resort reflect the gracious, open hospitality of a Hawaiian plantation home. Even the *kapa*-patterned stone floor at the entrance was custom-designed to capture a blend of classic and contemporary Hawaii—a theme continued in the lobby's raised ceiling with its mahogany battening and the wood panels on pillars.

The interior artwork was conceptualized with input from respected Hawaiian elders in order to make it sensitive and authentic to the site. From the beautiful grillwork to the feather *kahili* at the reception desk, the unique designs portray various traditional stories of the native Hawaiian people.

The luxuriously appointed one- and two-bed/bath units and three-bed/three-bath villas also offer a taste of Hawaiian style, complete with indoor–outdoor lanai areas providing for five-star sunsets on the Pacific Ocean or cool tropical breezes off the Waianae mountain range. The master suite features a king bed, private master bath with dual vanities, soaking tub, and separate shower.

North Shore, Oahu, Hawaii, USA

OCEAN VILLAS AT TURTLE BAY RESORT

Ideally located on the famed North Shore of Oahu, these oceanfront resort residences enjoy all the amenities of the 880-acre Turtle Bay Resort.

STATS
57 units in 7 buildings, studios to 4-bedroom villas; 4 restaurants, 3 lounges/bars; 880-acre site (entire resort)

FEATURES
Spa Luana; fitness center; 31,000-square-foot Pacific Rim Conference Center; 10-court tennis center; 2 landscaped pools including a 80-foot water slide; Arnold Palmer and George Fazio championship golf courses; retail shops; equestrian center; hiking and biking trails

KUDOS
Award for Best Design, New Construction, Upscale by *Lodging Hospitality*
Concrete Achievement Award by *Hawaiian Cement*

DON'T MISS
Observing the turtles that come to Kuilima Cove to feed on algae for 30 to 45 minutes every afternoon

GUESTS SAY
"Even though it's set in the most gorgeous and romantic location on the island, the villas are also ideal for families."

With the spectacular Pacific Ocean at your front door and a superb resort hotel at your back, Ocean Villas at Turtle Bay Resort offer all of the activities and all of the amenities you could want in a luxurious Hawaiian residence. Architects used Hawaiian-style roofs and added generous *lanai* (terrace) areas to maximize ocean viewing and capture the daylight from sunrise to sunset.

Each of the six innovative floor plans offers a seamless flow between indoor and out, conducive to Hawaiian-style entertaining. The choice of cool, quiet colors and the selection of elegant furnishings and finishes provide residents with a masterful blend of luxury and liveability. Ocean Villa residents have access to a private chef and exclusive use of a private pool, Jacuzzi, and courtyard in addition to all the Turtle Bay Resort amenities.

Kaanapali Beach, Maui, Hawaii, USA

SHERATON MAUI RESORT

A lava promontory 80 feet above the beach called Pu'u Keka'a, or Black Rock, dominates the hotel's remarkable site.

STATS
510 guestrooms and suites; 3 restaurants and 3 lounges/bars; 23-acre site

FEATURES
Fitness center; 17,000 square feet of ballroom, function, and meeting space; 3 tennis courts; 142-yard freshwater swimming lagoon; retail shops

KUDOS
Best Island Destination by *Condé Nast Traveler*
Top 25 Hotels and Resorts in Hawaii by *Travel+Leisure*
Golden Apple Award by Apple Vacations

DON'T MISS
The cliff diving ceremony at sundown set against the majestic sunset on Ka'anapali Beach

GUESTS SAY
"This is a beautiful hotel, on the nicest part of the beach, with a fantastic swimming pool."

The first hotel to be built on the Kaanapali coastline, the Sheraton Maui Resort continues to be a sought-after destination. Through renovations and additions, the buildings have retained their gracious curves, which are also mirrored in the curvilinear design of walkways, water features, and other amenities.

With the lobby located on the second floor, arriving guests have dramatic views of the ocean and Black Rock. Almost all of the guestrooms and suites directly face the Pacific Ocean, each with a private balcony for enjoying the view. Inside, the craftsmanship of old Hawaii reveals itself in lamps of bamboo design, patterns recalling block prints on *kapa*, and rattan chairs drawing on the peacock shapes of ancient thrones.

Guests can frolic in a 142-yard freshwater swimming lagoon of varying depths as it meanders through tropical gardens and under carved-wood bridges, and can also enjoy an outdoor spa set amid lava rock formations and waterfalls cascading from lush tropical flower beds.

Kohala Coast, Big Island, Hawaii, USA

THE FAIRMONT ORCHID

The indoor–outdoor guest experience suits this resort's tropical climate and oceanfront location.

STATS
540 guestrooms; 4 restaurants; 32-acre site

FEATURES
Spa Without Walls; fitness center; 30,000 square feet of indoor meeting space; 76,000 square feet of outdoor function space; 10-court tennis academy with exhibition court; 10,000-square-foot oceanfront swimming pool, lava whirlpools; 36-hole championship golf course; The Shops at Mauna Lani; amphitheater

KUDOS
Best Hotels in Hawaii by *Travel+Leisure*
Top 10 Hotels in Hawaii by *Condé Nast Traveler*

DON'T MISS
An outdoor massage in a *hale* that's cantilevered over the water, with a special floor window for gazing at the fish while on the treatment table

GUESTS SAY
"There's something about the place that you can't do justice to by itemizing all the various features; it's just beautifully magical."

A primary feature throughout The Fairmont Orchid is its openness to the natural elements: guestrooms have balconies with six-foot overhangs, interior courtyards open up to the sky, and public areas orient to views of the Kohala Coast and the Pacific.

Double-pitch roofs, colored tiles, koa wood banisters, and regional motifs—such as large sculpted pineapples used as anchoring posts for stairwells—reflect the local heritage in a blend of luxury and informality. Whether enjoying an oceanfront massage, a game of golf, an open-air dinner of Big Island cuisine, or simply a walk among the towering palms and waterfalls, the beauty of the Hawaiian Islands is a part of this resort experience.

The spa features ten island-inspired massage *hale*, or huts, nestled among a flowing network of waterfalls, streams, and lily ponds. The Spa Without Walls also extends to the water, where five private massage cabanas front the Pacific Ocean, allowing the gentle trade winds and awe-inspiring views to become part of every treatment.

THE ROYAL HAWAIIAN

Affectionately known as the "Pink Palace of the Pacific," the hotel has become an historic landmark on the world's most famous beach.

STATS
528 guestrooms and suites; restaurant, bar, and café; 15-acre site

FEATURES
Abhasa Waikiki Spa; fitness center/health club; 68,000 square feet of ballroom and function rooms; 10,000-square-foot outdoor function garden; business center; beach club; outdoor freshwater pool; retail arcade

DON'T MISS
The resort's oceanfront *luau*, where guests can enjoy an evening under the stars with Hawaiian melodies filling the air, a feast of foods from the islands, and a royal Polynesian extravaganza

GUESTS SAY
"This gem of a hotel is attractive in every sense, with its high archways, beautiful rugs and artwork, and gorgeous gardens with a variety of tropical plants. The lobby is both quiet and grand, with alcoves designed for conversation and relaxation."

Situated on the former site of the royal coconut grove and the summer home of Queen Kaahumanu, this legendary hotel was one of only two hotels in Waikiki when it opened in 1927 and has been host to many famous guests over the decades. With its original pink façade, vaulted archways that open onto secluded gardens, and spectacular beachfront location, The Royal Hawaiian is steeped in cultural authenticity and remains one the great hotels of the world.

In the historic building, handcrafted doors adorned with the Hawaiian coat of arms open to spacious guestrooms that offer the old-world charm of high ceilings, four-poster beds, and Queen Anne-style writing desks, along with all of today's modern amenities.

From the hotel's bars, restaurants, ballrooms, and function rooms, guests can enjoy Hawaiian food and entertainment while soaking in stunning views of the ocean, Diamond Head, and Waikiki Beach. The hotel's full-service spa offers treatments in secluded outdoor spaces within the hotel's gardens.

LATIN AMERICA CARIBBEAN

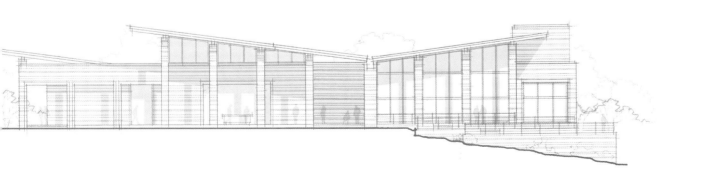

ATLANTIS, PARADISE ISLAND, BAHAMAS

The new luxury hotel and condominium within Atlantis, Paradise Island sit on a peninsula surrounded by lush landscaping and freshwater pools, overlooking two magnificent beaches.

STATS
600 suites in a 21-story hotel (The Cove); 497 residences in a 21-story condo-hotel (The Reef); 2 restaurants; 42-acre site (on the 171-acre Atlantis Resort)

FEATURES
30,000-square-foot Mandara Spa and fitness center; adult-only and family pools; luxury retail boutique; outdoor casino pavilion; Aquaventure; Dolphin Cay; access to all entertainment and recreation amenities of Atlantis

KUDOS
Most Unique Caribbean Hotel Experience by *Porthole Cruise*
#1 Best Mega Resort by *Caribbean Travel & Life*
Gold Key Award by *Meetings and Conventions*

DON'T MISS
The adult-only pool and 22 private cabanas offered to guests of The Cove

GUESTS SAY
"We loved the exclusivity of staying at The Cove and the benefits of being a part of Atlantis. The grounds are impeccable, the facilities are beautiful, and the spacious, lovely guestroom has a great view."

Representing the third phase of a multi-year collaboration between owner and architect that transformed an under-performing property into a world-class destination resort, these two newest buildings offer an unsurpassed level of privacy and sophistication within Atlantis' amenity-filled acreage. From the moment guests step into the lobby, they are transported by the commanding views of the ocean and beyond.

Guestrooms in The Cove range from 650 to 4,000 square feet, each with unobstructed views from floor-to-ceiling windows and private terraces.

Accommodations in The Reef feature 497 rooms in a 21-story condo-hotel. Residents have access to all Atlantis amenities including Aquaventure, a new 63-acre landscaped water experience, and Dolphin Cay, a state-of-the-art dolphin education center and interaction habitat.

The 9,000-square-foot, adults-only Ultra Pool is flanked by three smaller pool environments and private, butler-serviced cabanas that open directly to the beach. Guests can choose from a variety of settings and activities, including an outdoor gaming pavilion and a spa that sits across a glass bridge above a water garden.

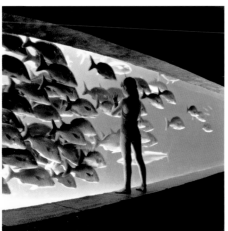

Mexico City, Mexico

FOUR SEASONS HOTEL MEXICO, D.F.

Situated on the Paseo de la Reforma, near Chapultepec Park and the National Museum of Anthropology and History, the hotel is a secluded and private retreat in the center of one of the world's largest cities.

STATS
240 guestrooms, including 40 suites;
2 restaurants and lounge; 1.75-acre site

FEATURES
Spa; health club; 13,000 square feet of meeting/
banquet/conference space; business center;
rooftop pool and sundeck

KUDOS
Best Hotel in Mexico, Central and South America
by *Travel+Leisure*

DON'T MISS
The Weekend Cultural Program, which includes
scheduled visits to Mexico City's major sites—art
historians lead informative tours every Saturday
and Sunday morning

GUESTS SAY
"It's a cliché repeated by others who come to this
hotel, but it really is an 'oasis of peace' in the
center of Mexico City. Once you're inside the Four
Seasons, it's like you're a world away."

The design of this hotel is derived from a blending of Spanish Colonial and historic French influences. One element that contributes to the feeling of privacy is the hotel's low, coffered, formal carriage entrance. The entry—with its stone paving, glass lanterns, and mullioned doors—opens into the lobby, which, in turn, opens out to a serene, central landscaped courtyard and surrounding colonnade.

The large courtyard serves as the hotel's gathering spot for dining and meetings, and also provides natural light and green views for the guestrooms. While the inner courtyard and exterior façade borrow from Mexico's long heritage of Spanish Colonial architecture, the historic French influence emerges in significant decorative elements such as the wrought-iron scrollwork of banisters and the high, arched windows.

Costos Banderas, Nayarit, Mexico

FOUR SEASONS RESORT PUNTA MITA

The hotel is approached through a cobblestone entryway and open courtyard that are reminiscent of the great haciendas.

Like a cluster of elegant residences nestled into the hillside, tile-roofed casitas of one- to three-stories house guestrooms and suites, each with an ocean view. Even the main building, which features an open-sided traditional thatched *palapa*, is a low-rise structure designed in the vernacular of tropical Mexico.

While every guestroom offers breathtaking views of the ocean from a large terrace or balcony, most suites also feature a private plunge pool.

A cultural center with a range of fascinating programs and activities is available on site and other features of the resort—including a full-service spa, tennis center, a range of pools, two beaches, dining options, and private championship golf course—provide the perfect getaway without venturing beyond the resort. There is also a 100-unit vacation ownership community on the site, which has its own Resort Club Community Center.

HACIENDA DEL MAR RESORT & SPA

This resort succeeds at blending old Mexico charm with luxury resort accommodations and amenities.

STATS
270 guestrooms, including 31 suites and 234 vacation ownership villas; 5 restaurants and 5 bars; 28-acre site

FEATURES
Cactus Spa; fitness center; 18,000-square-foot conference facility; Hacienda Ballroom; business center; tennis facility; 4 swimming pools; 18-hole Desert Course and neighboring 18-hole Ocean Course (Jack Nicklaus design); Mexican chapel

KUDOS
One of the Top 100 Golf Courses Worldwide (Ocean Course), by *Condé Nast Traveler*
The 100 Greatest Golf Courses Outside the United States (Ocean Course), by *Golf Digest*
Five Star Diamond Award (Pitahayas restaurant), by American Academy of Hospitality Sciences

DON'T MISS
Whale-watching, snorkeling, canopy rides (rip lines, high over canyons)

GUESTS SAY
"This resort is heaven on earth. The architecture and landscaping create a calming atmosphere; the grounds, especially at night, are incredibly romantic."

A renowned destination for golf, this Latin American paradise is also known for its world-class sport fishing and the marvels of the Sea of Cortez, home to migration whales, dolphins, sea turtles, and hundreds of fish and marine species.

Designed in the style of a colonial Mexican village, a central building serves as the resort's focal point and is surrounded by villas, courtyards, pathways, and fountains. The resort's villas are spread across 26 buildings with heights ranging from two to five stories. All of them offer panoramic views, terraces, patios, balconies, and seamless transitions between indoors and out. Cut-stone pathways and fountains bordered with native greenery connect the various activity centers of this resort community. The main infinity pool appears to merge into the Sea of Cortez and is one of four swimming options for guests and residents.

MIDDLE EAST
AFRICA

Dubai, United Arab Emirates

EMIRATES HILLS VILLA ESTATES

Each property in Emirates Hills is different from every other, but all offer an unrivalled level of luxury, complete with private pools and views of the world-class Montgomerie Championship Golf Course.

STATS
400 residential units ranging in size from 15,000 to 40,000 square feet (Phase 1); 3,000 residential units (Phase 2); 12 restaurants; 400-acre site (Phase 1); 2,000-acre site (total)

FEATURES
Spa; gymnasium; conference center; tennis courts; swimming pool; 18-hole championship golf course designed by Montgomerie and Muirhead; golf clubhouse; golf academy; par-three teaching course and another 18-hole golf course; sales office; future schools; mosques; civic and commercial office buildings

DON'T MISS
The par-three 13th hole designed in the shape of the UAE and the largest single golfing green in the world

GUESTS SAY
"The landscaping and exquisite exteriors make Emirates Hills Villas one of the most sought after and prestigious master-planned communities in the world."

Emirates Hills Villas belong to a community of luxury estates situated in the prestigious Emirates Hills Golf Resort, on the outskirts of Dubai. Design of the villas successfully combines contemporary ideas of resort living with the traditional beliefs and practices of the local populace. The architectural character reflects regional and traditional forms, while the detailing evokes local influences.

Every residence in the Emirates Hills Villas has two distinct zones of social interaction, based upon the traditional Islamic practice of separating the men's living areas *(majlis)* from the women's and children's living areas. Separate entrances are also provided so that men and women can circulate in complete privacy. Likewise, the gardens and terraces at the rear serve both formal functions and casual family functions, with distinct outdoor spaces that can be separated and screened from each other. The villas also incorporate contemporary Western elements such as gourmet kitchens and casual, open spaces for the family.

Abu Dhabi, United Arab Emirates

EMIRATES PALACE

Built in the style of a majestic palace, the elaborate and luxurious design combines a conference centre, guest palace, and two luxury hotel wings to create the finest example of a grand civic building in the United Arab Emirates.

STATS
302 grand rooms plus 92 suites; 12 restaurants and lounges; 247-acre site

FEATURES
Anatara Spa, including Moroccan Hammam facility; 2 fitness centers; conference center with 40 conference rooms, ballroom for 2,400 people, auditorium for 1,100; business center; media center; 1-mile private beach; 4 tennis courts; relaxation and activity pools; retail shops; PADI diving center; Energy Zone; Sarab Land for children; helicopter pad

KUDOS
Worlds Leading Conference Hotel by World Travel Awards
Worlds Leading Suite by World Travel Awards
Best 5-Star Leisure Hotel by MENA Travel Awards

DON'T MISS
The Palace's collection of 1,002 chandeliers made with Swarovski's premier Strauss crystals

GUESTS SAY
"This has to be the most amazing hotel in the world. It's as close as you'll get to feeling like royalty; truly a palace."

The 114 domes that sit atop the main and ancillary buildings proudly reference Arabian culture, while the color choices reflect the shades of sand found in the Arabian Desert. Modern techniques such as etching and casting were used to apply traditional patterns to the Palace's marble, granite, and stone façade.

The Guest Palace houses accommodations for 22 Heads of State, including six suites on the uppermost floor that are dedicated to the Gulf Cooperation Council. The two hotel wings host international conference speakers and delegates, as well as leisure guests who appreciate the height of luxury.

The Palace Conference Centre is the most luxurious and technologically advanced meeting facility in the region. On the lower levels of the Palace, guests can partake of culinary options from across the globe, choosing from 12 exquisite dining venues. The leisure pool is perfect for relaxation, while the adventure pool features water slides and a jet-propelled lazy river. The entire complex sits on acres of landscaped gardens alongside Abu Dhabi's most beautiful, private sandy beach.

Heliopolis, Cairo, Egypt

FAIRMONT TOWERS HELIOPOLIS

The hotel is built around a magnificent atrium featuring tropical gardens, palm trees, a flowing stream, and comfortable seating areas throughout.

With a location convenient both to the city and to popular tourist attractions, the Fairmont Towers Heliopolis appeals equally to business and leisure travellers, and offers unique world-class facilities. Designed with energy efficiency and security in mind, the hotel includes a luxurious indoor garden and pools that sit above a sunken arrangement of elegant meeting facilities—the largest and best equipped in Cairo.

A Red Sea design theme in the conference venue incorporates elements that evoke water, sand, and coral. Water features and dramatic lighting vary the mood of the public spaces during the day and night. Elsewhere, the theme is based upon Heliopolis—the city of the sun—with radiating lines in the structure, finishes, and lighting that evoke sunbeams and silhouettes. In the guestrooms and public areas, richly colored woods and subtle earth tones combine and contrast with vibrant colors of decorative glass and lighting in a design that is both contemporary and reflective of the region.

Guests indulging in the spa enter the facility across a bridge over a sunken garden and head to either the dry therapy or hydrotherapy wing. Those dining at the gourmet restaurant are seated at tables atop wooden pontoons over the water.

Dubai, United Arab Emirates

FOUR SEASONS GOLF CLUB DUBAI FESTIVAL CITY

The focal point for the Al Badia championship golf course is the breathtaking clubhouse—a unique and dramatic structure whose innovative design emulates the swirl of the golfer's swing and offers a festive atmosphere.

STATS
3 restaurants; atrium lounge; 85-acre site

FEATURES
Sauna and steam rooms; 30,257 square feet of banquet facilities and meeting rooms; 18-hole Robert Trent Jones II golf course; golf academy; Science and Motion putting laboratory; comprehensive golf shop

DON'T MISS
The renowned 18-hole championship Al Badia golf course, designed by Robert Trent Jones II, which features a desert oasis theme

GUESTS SAY
"Elegant ambiance, beautiful art and architecture, and spectacular views."

The clubhouse is designed in a wrapping form of golden roofs, stone, and blue glass, culminating in a central atrium punctuated with water features. The lower roofs sweep around the terrace, providing shade and reinforcing the Al Badia theme, which translates to "Land of the Bedouins." Arriving at the entry to the clubhouse, visitors are greeted by a framed vista over the golf course and the lakes.

Three restaurants, with seating both indoors and out, offer sweeping panoramic views to downtown Dubai and the surrounding golf course. At Quattro, guests gaze at cascading waterfalls and the 18th hole. At Blades, diners enjoys views of the 9th green from the base of the soaring 89-foot outer blue-glass wall that curves around the building in the shape of a blade. And at Spikes, golfers overlook the practice facilities and enjoy the impressive Sheikh Zayed Road skyline. The Tee Lounge offers a stylish place for meeting beneath the atrium's swirling glass roof.

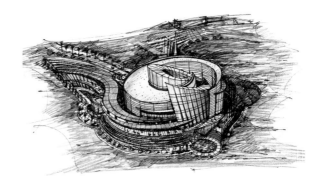

Amman, Jordan

GRAND HYATT AMMAN

The hotel was designed to set a new standard of luxury for city center hotels throughout the region.

Acknowledging the importance of the building as a civic landmark, the hotel is designed with local stone to reflect the character of Amman and the unique land of Jordan. Traditional Arab textures and patterns can be seen in a range of finishes such as those in the courtyard and on the roof terraces, and the architects have also echoed the images of the famed Petra Rock as a vertical cleft above the entry lobby.

The 15-story building encloses a tiered, open courtyard. Three public levels attract both international guests and local visitors to the meeting space, ballroom, restaurants, and retail mezzanine.

Wolmar, Flic en Flac, Mauritius, Africa

HILTON MAURITIUS RESORT & SPA

This resort is set on the coast of a beautiful island in the Indian Ocean, where guests can enjoy invigorating water sports or indulge in relaxing spa treatments.

On the western shore of the Island of Mauritius, protected by a lagoon and bordered by white sand beaches, the resort is perfectly integrated into lush vegetation. The luxurious property was master-planned to preserve the existing trees, with the rooms arranged around lush flora in small pavilions facing the sunset and the sea.

There are pools, gardens, and walkways to discover, and guests can also visit the island's own bird park and crocodile farm. Guests seeking the utmost in relaxation can find it in any one of the locally inspired spa treatments at one of the largest spas in the region.

MÖVENPICK RESORT & RESIDENCE AQABA

With its elegant Arabesque design, this resort and residence offers sunset views of Sinai, the Red Sea, and the Gulf of Aqaba.

The resort is immediately adjacent to the ruins of the ancient trading port of Ayla, now part of Aqaba, the second city of Jordan and the oldest historical city on the Red Sea. Surrounded by magnificent red mountains and a turquoise sea edged with sandy beaches, the destination's archaeological sites include a Mamluk Fort and the remains of the oldest purpose-built Christian church in the world.

A sensitive effort was made in the design of the Mövenpick Resort & Residence to integrate Jordan's heritage and the traditional hospitality of the region with the amenities of a modern resort. The main hotel building is on the landward side of the city's corniche, with a pedestrian bridge that includes a swimming pool and links the western gate of the old city wall to the beach, residences, and resort facilities.

MÖVENPICK RESORT & SPA DEAD SEA

Drawing on the history and culture of Jordan, this luxury resort evokes the rich heritage of its ancient location.

STATS
358 guestrooms, including 57 suites; 10 restaurants and lounges; 16-acre site

FEATURES
Full-service spa with 24 treatment rooms; fitness center; indoor and outdoor function space; 500-seat amphitheater; 5 swimming pools; 2 tennis courts

KUDOS
50 Greatest Views in the World by *The Sunday Times Travel*
4th Best Overseas Destination Spa by *Condé Nast Traveler*

DON'T MISS
Following up a dip in the Dead Sea with a swim in the resort's heated pool

GUESTS SAY
"A fantastic, authentic hotel with real charm and five-star comforts. The village design is a constant reminder of the rich and beautiful heritage of the Middle East."

For this resort, the architects drew inspiration from the region's natural environment, notably working with the sloping, boulder-strewn site rather than against it. An ornate main building, surrounded by various groupings of guestrooms, recalls the streets of old Jerusalem. Restaurants, shops, and artisan workshops comprise the resort's village, and the grounds also feature fountains, gardens, and a courtyard typical of small Jordanian towns. The design inspiration for these older-style buildings came from Arabic idioms and local materials, offering guests an opportunity to experience the local culture.

At 1,320 feet below sea level, there is virtually no ultra-violet radiation to cause sunburn, making this location perfectly suited to the wellness and spa markets. In light of lengthy stays, the guestrooms are spacious and each has a shaded, private terrace or a balcony.

The hotel's Zara Spa is one of the most sophisticated and extensive spa facilities in the Middle East, with more than 60 treatments and programs, including hydrotherapy pools with water from the Dead Sea.

Hurghada, Red Sea, Egypt

MÖVENPICK RESORT & SPA EL GOUNA

Nestled near the tip of El Gouna, and located directly on the beach with spectacular views of the Red Sea, this resort is set amid tranquil lagoons and lush gardens to blend with the natural environment.

All of the resort's guestrooms feature a balcony or terrace, with sea, lagoon, or garden views. Guests can choose from a range of recreational activities on site, which include a dive center, kite-surfing station, and a variety of landscaped swimming pools. Dining options take full advantage of the site's unique location overlooking the crystal blue sea and incorporate a range of regional delicacies. Those looking for further relaxation will find it in the resort's spa, which offers a wide range of beauty and wellness treatments inspired by a fusion of techniques from the East and West.

Only minutes away, guests can explore El Gouna's main fare or choose to play the nearby 18-hole Gene Bates and Fred Couples-designed golf course. An exciting range of day excursions is also available to guests, which include visits to historical sites of Egypt, including the temples of Luxor and the great Pyramids of Gizeh in Cairo, or adventures through the desert on a camel, quad bike, or sand buggy.

Belle Mare, Mauritius

ONE&ONLY
LE SAINT GÉRAN RESORT

Located on the tip of a 60-acre private peninsula in the Indian Ocean, the resort is a sanctuary of refinement and serenity.

STATS
148 junior suites, 14 ocean suites, 1 villa; 3 resturaunts and 2 bars; 60-acre site

FEATURES
Givenchy Spa; salon; fitness facility; conference center and boardroom; business center; Peter Burwash International Tennis Club; pool; 9-hole Gary Player golf course and golf academy; marina boat house

KUDOS
Highest Commitment to Quality Score Overall by *Leading Hotels of the World*
Top 10 Best Spas—Africa, Middle East & Indian Ocean by *Condé Nast Traveler*
Best Hotel in the World for Food by *Condé Nast Traveler*

DON'T MISS
Activities at the water sports center, including snorkeling, trips on the glass-bottom boat, sailing on the hotel's catamarans, windsurfing, kayaking, and a water ski slalom course

GUESTS SAY
"Straight out of a postcard, both the setting and the hotel."

Extensive remodeling did not sacrifice the original style and character of the "Grande Dame" of Mauritius. Immortalised in Bernardin de Saint Pierre's novel *Paul et Virginie*, the resort is located near the site of the historic Le Saint Géran shipwreck. The hotel features terraced and balconied rooms, all facing out privately to the Indian Ocean, and suites that offer their own beach access and al fresco showers. A combination of island colors and materials contributes to the old-world elegance of the resort.

Under the calm sway of thousands of coconut palms, immaculate gardens run down to the edge of the pure white sand beach, which seamlessly wraps around the peninsula for over a mile, and a sheltered lagoon provides tranquil waters for an array of water sports. With its private lap pool inside a tropical garden, the internationally acclaimed Givenchy Spa is designed to blend with the resort's architecture and unique location.

Serengeti, Tanzania, Africa

SASAKWA LODGE

This ultra-luxurious hilltop resort, with its wide wraparound verandas, offers awe-inspiring vistas over the private 350,000-acre Grumeti Game Reserve, an ideal location for viewing the annual migration of wildebeest, zebra, and gazelle.

STATS
7 free-standing cottages, including 6 suites and a luxury villa; restaurant and bar; 297,000-acre site

FEATURES
Spa; business center; 2 tennis courts; infinity pool; Colonial Trading Post; library; wine room; billiards room; sports pavilion; equestrian center

KUDOS
The World's 100 Ultimate Escapes by Robb Report
Global Vision Award by Travel+Leisure
15 to Watch by Travel+Leisure

DON'T MISS
Taking a splash in the lodge's infinity-edge pool overlooking the Serengeti after a massage and hot-stone therapy treatment in the cliff-edge spa

GUESTS SAY
"The outstanding facilities and stunning views of the plains are truly inspiring."

Sasakwa's free-standing cottages, designed in the style of a turn-of-the-century East African colonial manor home, feature wood paneling, antique furnishings, and infinity-edge pools set in private gardens. The concept was inspired by a desire to merge existing built and natural environments, matching the colors, materials, and building heights with the tone of the landscape. The goal of the master plan was to give the land an untouched feel, so existing trees were carefully relocated—no mature trees were cut down—and most of the plants used in the design are indigenous to the area.

Comprising one- to four-bedroom suites in seven cottages, the resort can accommodate up to 30 people. As sustainability is a key element of the project, the construction was carried out by tradespersons from local villages with materials from surrounding areas.

Muscat, Oman

SHANGRI-LA'S
BARR AL JISSAH RESORT & SPA

Since buried archaeological treasures were uncovered here, every consideration has been taken to preserve and enhance the site's historical value. The resort's beach, listed as one of the world's rare breeding coves for turtles, is a true ecological wonder.

The country's first truly integrated destination resort includes three separate and distinct luxury hotels, each designed to reflect Oman's cultural heritage, linked together by more than 1,600 feet of swimming pools. The design team drew inspiration from the historic, isolated beauty of the site and the ancient castles, palaces, cities, towns, and mud-brick villages that embody the Sultanate's unique regional identity.

Al Waha, *The Oasis*, sits in a separate *wadi* (valley) to the southern end of the resort and caters primarily to the leisure traveler and to families, offering spacious and contemporary rooms with games and entertainment for younger guests. Al Bandar, *The Town*, is the heart of the resort and features award-winning restaurants, upscale retail, a ballroom, and meeting rooms centered around a beachside piazza. Al Husn, *The Castle*, provides the highest level of discreet, luxurious, and elegant hospitality in an exclusive six-star setting elevated more than 65 feet over the rest of the resort on a breathtaking cliff top.

Red Sea, Egypt

SHERATON SOMA BAY

Soma Bay is an all-year sunshine destination built on a peninsula surrounded by the azure waters of the Red Sea. The resort itself sits on 2,296 feet of beachfront property and is flanked by the serene backdrop of desert mountains.

STATS
275 guestrooms, including 35 suites;
3 restaurants and 4 bars; 42-acre site

FEATURES
Thalasso & Wellness Center; health club; 5,758 square feet of conference and meeting facilities; 3 tennis courts, squash court, croquet court; 8,611-square-foot Aquatonic Pool; 18-hole Gary Player Cascades championship golf course; Soma Bay Marina; diving center; kite surf center

KUDOS
Egypt's Leading Golf Resort
by World Travel Awards
Holly Award by Touristik Union International

DON'T MISS
Soma Bay, which provides a unique diving and snorkeling experience; just a few minutes from the shore, seven pillars of coral rise 65 feet from the sandy bottom

GUESTS SAY
"One of the most incredible lobbies that I have ever seen. The rooms, the services, the landscape ... everything was like a dream come true."

The resort's dramatic architecture was inspired by Luxor's magnificent Karnak Temple. Ancient iconography is integrated into the styling of both interior and exterior spaces; and cool, green areas and water features are incorporated into the carefully designed courtyards.

Guestrooms and suites reflect the simplicity and tranquility of the resort's surroundings and are decorated in soothing pastel colors and modern oak furnishings. Each overlooks lagoons and desert gardens with views across Soma Bay to the mountains of the Eastern Desert.

Guests can enjoy a variety of different activities including a spectacular pool, world-famous diving and snorkeling, hydrotherapy treatments, and a championship golf course designed by Gary Player to incorporate stunning views of the Red Sea.

THE PALACE AT ONE&ONLY ROYAL MIRAGE

Challenging the status quo of sleek, contemporary high-rise hotels in Dubai, the Royal Mirage was patterned after a traditional Arabian home.

STATS
246 guestrooms and suites; 4 restaurants, a lounge and a nightclub; 25-acre site

FEATURES
Deluxe health and beauty salon; fitness studio; conference and banqueting areas; 3 tennis courts; swimming pools; boutique shops

KUDOS
Best Leisure/Resort Hotel in the Middle East by *Business Traveler*
Middle East & North Africa Hotel of the Year by DEPA Hotel Awards
Tagine, "Highly Recommended, Best North African Restaurant" by *Time Out* Restaurant Awards
Top Hotel Spa in Africa, Middle East, Indian Ocean by *Condé Nast Traveller*

DON'T MISS
The details that go into helping you relax, unwind, and immerse yourself in the experience, right down to the Arabian slippers next to your bed

GUESTS SAY
"The quiet ambience and the understated opulence of the architecture make this our favorite hotel. It's an oasis in the otherwise frenetic Dubai."

Thirteen hundred palm trees encircle this splendid palace, while courtyards, waterways, and terraces ensure that the views and beach environment are primary focal points. The design inspiration for the resort is based on the rich heritage of the region, and traditional Arabic elements—such as tile floors, curving archways, and diffused lighting from lanterns and torches throughout—imbue the destination with a strong sense of place. Guestroom bathing suites are complete with vaulted ceilings, gilded mirrors, and an arched opening that frames the tub. Within a tranquil haven, guests can enjoy a range of settings such as an Arabian court, a Health and Beauty Institute, temperature-controlled swimming pools, and dining options that include a rooftop terrace.

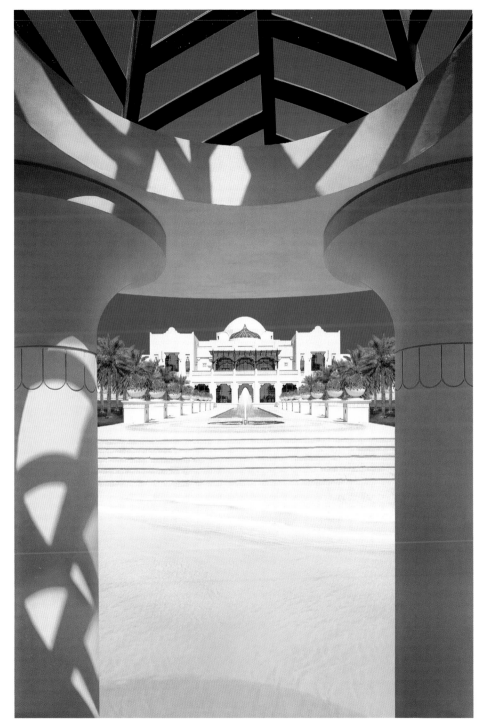

Sun City, South Africa

THE PALACE OF THE LOST CITY

A fictional account of a mythical lost kingdom, newly rediscovered, became the design theme for a luxury hotel of unprecedented opulence and originality.

STATS
322 guestrooms, including 16 suites;
6 restaurants and lounges; 68-acre site

FEATURES
Spa; fitness center; conference center; business center; tennis courts; Olympic-size pool; two 18-hole Gary Player golf courses; retail; Valley of Waves water adventure park; 62 acres of lakes, rivers and jungles

KUDOS
The Best Hotel in the World
by *Lodging Hospitality*
World's Best Hotels and Resorts Gold List
by *Condé Nast Traveler*
Award of Merit
by Institute of South Africa Architects

DON'T MISS
The 13th hole of The Lost City Golf Course, where 38 crocodiles inhabit the water hazard

GUESTS SAY
"Architecturally, this hotel takes your breath away. It's hard to use anything but superlatives in describing The Palace."

Surrounded by water and approached across an entrance bridge, The Palace, with its vast arches and domed towers, seems to rise from its surroundings. In every monumental feature and in every minute detail, The Palace is designed to replicate a "rediscovered" ancient and mythical royal residence through a series of legends written by the architects. Throughout the resort, there is a richness of detail inspired by Africa's natural vegetation and wildlife.

A six-story rotunda, conceived as the royal entrance chamber, overlooks a magnificent palatial lobby lounge. Guestrooms open to a five-story space crowned by a skylit ceiling that is supported by structural stone columns and accented with simulated tusk mullions.

Revitalizing the local economy, the design team engaged over 2,000 local artists and artisans to create mosaic floors, hand-painted murals and custom-designed furnishings and finishes. Highlighting the fantasy environment is a landscape of rare and exotic vegetation that includes more than 1.6 million trees and a water adventure park.

NORTH AMERICA

St. Charles, Missouri, USA

AMERISTAR CASINO ST. CHARLES

At this gaming entertainment destination, visitors can enjoy the vast casino and its adjoining entertainment-packed streetscape before retreating to the property's luxurious hotel and spa.

STATS
397 suites; 8 restaurants and 9 bars; 58-acre site

FEATURES
7,000-square-foot spa; 20,000 square feet of conference center and Discovery Ballroom space; business center; indoor–outdoor pool; gift shop; 130,000-square-foot-casino; video arcade; 80,000-square-foot entertainment complex; 2 live entertainment venues

KUDOS
Best Casino in Missouri by Casino Player

DON'T MISS
Soaking in a whirlpool tub overlooking the city through a custom bay window in your suite

GUESTS SAY
"This is where luxury meets fun."

In homage to the historical architecture of the area, the hotel's exterior has been painstakingly detailed to incorporate the time-worn quality of aged brick and decorative ornamental cast moldings. The hotel's sweeping two-story lobby greets guests with scenic views of the Missouri River, also showcased from the sunken living room of each spacious suite.

High-end finishes—including rare onyx imported from China and handcrafted glass tile from New Mexico—also distinguish the hotel's conference center, which hosts events and meetings that call upon the center's signature culinary team and state-of-the-art audiovisual capabilities. When work is not on the agenda, guests can indulge in the hotel's full-service spa designed as a relaxing water-themed environment.

A variety of dynamic restaurants, shops, and entertainment venues—all designed to complement the casino—make this a leading tourist attraction in the St. Louis area.

AMERISTAR KANSAS CITY CASINO HOTEL & ENTERTAINMENT CENTER

This Midwest entertainment mecca offers something for everyone—twin floating casinos, 11 restaurants, a 1,384-seat theater, 18 movie screens— and a luxury hotel.

STATS
184 guestrooms and suites; 11 dining venues; 183-acre site

FEATURES
Star Club, a private players' lounge; Star Pavilion for national headliners; Depot #9 for regional acts; Casino Cabaret; 18-screen theater; Hi-Vi video arcade; 2,660-car parking structure; gift shop; Kids' Quest

KUDOS
Best Casino by *Kansas City Magazine*
Favorite Casino Hotel by *Midwest Gaming & Travel*
Best Overall Casino Hotel by *Casino Player* and *Strictly Slots*

DON'T MISS
Playing poker with several hundred of your closest friends

GUESTS SAY
"The guestroom is a beautiful place to come back to and relax."

The client wanted this property to be known for more than just its state-of-the-art casino, so designers renovated the hotel, incorporating custom finishes and furnishings for luxury and comfort. Beyond the dramatic new lobby enveloped in layers of color and texture, guestrooms feature distinctive carpeting, furniture, and light fixtures, all in a rich, espresso-toned color scheme. European-style bedding and plasma-screen televisions, along with luxurious bathrooms and amenities, create an oasis of comfort and a quiet retreat from the action.

Ameristar Casino Kansas City is one of the largest and most impressive casinos in the country, boasting more than 3,000 slot and video poker machines and over 100 table games, with one of the grandest poker rooms in the American Midwest. The casino and hotel have earned numerous awards.

Bend, Oregon, USA

BROKEN TOP GOLF CLUBHOUSE

With its great room, members' lounge, and meeting facilities, this clubhouse serves as a living room for the entire residential resort community of Broken Top.

STATS
27,000-square-foot clubhouse; dining room and members' grill; 500-acre site

FEATURES
Exercise room; 4 tennis courts; swimming complex; 18-hole championship golf course; pro shop; locker room

KUDOS
Grand Award by Builder's Choice
Award of Merit by Gold Nugget Awards
Honorable Mention by American Institute of Architects (AIA) Orange County

DON'T MISS
Breathtaking views of the seven Cascade peaks and the 6-acre Broken Top Lake

GUESTS SAY
"The view from the clubhouse across the small lake, with the mountains in the background, was fabulous!"

Natural materials used for the clubhouse design—most prominently wood and stone—complement the rugged beauty of the site and make the structure appear to be rooted to a boulder- and brush-covered plateau. The clubhouse is situated with a 360-degree exposure to the lake, golf course, forestland, and Cascade peaks in the distance.

The staircase was created from natural boulders, one of which forms the base of a 30-foot-high fireplace. An element that makes the clubhouse particularly appealing as a year-round retreat is a sense of openness achieved with high ceilings, expansive glass, and long views.

Walt Disney World® Resort, Lake Buena Vista, Florida, USA

DISNEY'S GRAND FLORIDIAN RESORT & SPA

This stately resort offers elegance and charm that is reminiscent of the grand old Victorian hotels along the Florida coast.

STATS
867 guestrooms and suites; 7 restaurants and lounges; 50-acre site

FEATURES
Grand Floridian Spa and Health Club; 40,000-square-foot conference center including 2 ballrooms and 16 meeting rooms; business center; 2 tennis courts; 8,000-square-foot pool; 3 championship golf courses with a 9-hole executive course; retail shops; marina with water sports and yacht; monorail station; arcade; wedding chapel; child care facility; white-sand beach

KUDOS
Honor Award by American Institute of Architects

Top 10 Best Hotels in the Continental U.S. and Canada by *Travel+Leisure*

Best Resort Hotels in North America by 20,000 travel agents

DON'T MISS
The nightly water parade on the lagoon that features lighted floats passing by the resort as songs and images brighten the night sky

GUESTS SAY
"The ambience of this grand hotel is magical."

Victorian architecture is in abundance here with towers, dormers, cupolas, exposed gable trusses, and band-sawed gingerbread styling. A Victorian-style monorail station serves as the hotel's entry and leads into a breathtaking lobby that ascends five stories and is capped with illuminated stained-glass domes. Glistening chandeliers, an aviary, and a grand piano add to the lobby's lavish ambience. An open-cage elevator transports guests to the second-floor shops and restaurants.

Four- and five-story buildings of gleaming white-clapboard siding, red-shingled roofs, fairytale turrets, and intricate latticework are arranged village-style. Impeccably maintained and perfectly manicured grounds meander among the buildings, and a wide, white-sand beach completes the scenario for this luxuriously fun resort.

Westlake Village, California, USA

FOUR SEASONS HOTEL WESTLAKE VILLAGE

Located less than an hour from Los Angeles and Burbank, the residential design and serene surroundings of this hotel provide a unique and luxurious retreat.

The atmosphere of the hotel is influenced by its relationship to the adjacent diagnostic health and wellness facility, California WellBeing Institute. Spacious guestrooms and suites—all with high ceilings, hardwood floors, and elegant appointments—welcome guests with a warm residential ambience. Many offer views of the hotel's gardens and waterfall through dramatic floor-to-ceiling windows.

The innovative spa and fitness center are designed to incorporate the latest in health and wellness offerings, while a meditation lawn, exercise path, and Mediterranean-inspired lap pool encourage relaxation as well as recreation. With generous indoor and outdoor meeting and event space, this is the area's premier location for corporate gatherings and special occasions. The facilities are complemented by the latest audio-visual technology and include a state-of-the-art television studio—all of it wrapped in acres of lush, exotic landscaping and gardens.

Carlsbad, California, USA

FOUR SEASONS RESORT AVIARA

The resort is built on a plateau overlooking both the Pacific Ocean and the Batiquitos Lagoon—protected wetlands that are home to the more than 130 species of birds, which provided the inspiration for the name "Aviara."

STATS
329 guestrooms, including 44 suites and 240 villa units; 4 restaurants and 2 bars; 200-acre site

FEATURES
Spa; José Eber Salon; fitness center; banquet/meeting rooms; business center; 6 tennis courts; family pool with adjoining children's water playground, quiet pool, and separate pool in each villa village; Arnold Palmer-designed 18-hole golf course; driving range; clubhouse with golf shop; shopettes; game room

KUDOS
Gold List by *Condé Nast Traveler*
World's Best Business Hotels by *Travel+Leisure*
Top 50 U.S. Mainland Resorts by *Condé Nast Traveler*

DON'T MISS
The adults-only quiet pool with soft music underwater

GUESTS SAY
"All I can say is 'Wow, what a stunning resort!' The attention to detail is amazing."

This world-class hotel and the vacation ownership villas surrounding it are designed as an adaptation of Santa Barbara Mission architecture, adopting the white stucco and red-tile roofs typical of the style. Enormous windows frame outdoor spaces, and muted, natural colors and finishes create a luxurious, warm, and inviting setting.

A porte-cochère and marble-floored promenade welcome visitors to the resort, and each of the deluxe guestrooms features an oversized bathroom and a landscaped terrace or balcony with stunning views of the lagoon, golf course, or ocean.

Four Seasons Resort Aviara was designed as an integral part of a 1,000-acre master-planned resort and residential community. The 240 villa units are arranged around the hotel in three villages, each with its own amenities.

The award-winning golf course follows the natural topography of three valleys and adheres to the ecological regulations of the wildlife sanctuary.

Carefree, Arizona, USA

GOLDEN DOOR SPA AT THE BOULDERS RESORT

Designed with elements of Feng Shui and exuding a Zen-like ambience, the resort offers its guests a memorable spa experience in the dramatic natural setting of the surrounding Sonoran Desert.

STATS
33,000-square-foot spa

FEATURES
25 treatment spaces; 2,000-square-foot fitness center with full stress center; cardio–weight room; movement studio; private locker rooms with steam rooms, saunas, and Japanese baths; outdoor swimming pool with heated whirlpool; full-service beauty salon; retail shop

KUDOS
Best Overall Spa in the U.S. by *Travel+Leisure*
Top 10 Spas in North America by *Spa Finder*
America's Best Hotel & Resort Spas by *Mobil Travel Guide*

DON'T MISS
The Labyrinth, a path to tranquility inspired by ancient Hopi medicine wheels, and The Watsu, offering an underwater "back-to-the-womb" experience

GUESTS SAY
"Golden Door Spa is spectacular! The spa is world-class and the setting is dramatic and unique."

The spa was designed to wrap around the northern base of the resort's signature boulder monument, forming the entry to the sprawling grounds of the resort and residential property. A striking feature of the spa is its high windows, which offer guests stunning panoramic views of the unique local environment.

A full menu of soothing treatments is offered in the spa's 25 treatment spaces, which include Vichy treatment rooms, an interior rock-and-sand garden, outdoor patios, and a 700-foot spa suite complete with its own access, whirlpool, outdoor fireplace, steam showers, data port, and television. Other signature features include the traditional Japanese *furo* bath, a meditation labyrinth, a circular café and tea room, and a heated swimming pool encircled by ancient boulders and towering cacti.

HYATT REGENCY HUNTINGTON BEACH RESORT & SPA

Perched along the historic Pacific Coast Highway, the resort offers dramatic ocean views and an atmosphere of casual elegance that is quintessential Southern California.

The design for this premier oceanfront resort and conference facility is reminiscent of an Andalusian village, a region in southern Spain known for its natural beauty and classic Mediterranean architecture. The collection of Mission-inspired low-rise buildings, graceful arches, and open-air courtyards all frame unobstructed views of the Pacific coastline.

Outdoor fireplaces, majestic fountains, and lush landscaping accentuate the resort's garden environment. Guests can relax by the lagoon-style pool or unwind at the secluded spa grotto and Pacific Waters Spa. They can also take advantage of wonderful restaurant options on the property or explore miles of white sandy beaches accessed via the pedestrian bridge.

The conference center, located at the west end of the resort, is complete with its own porte-cochère, villa-style lobby, and three ocean-view ballrooms.

Henderson, Nevada, USA

LAKE LAS VEGAS RESORT

Situated only 17 miles from the Las Vegas Strip is a deluxe resort styled after a Mediterranean town, where guests can enjoy year-round golf in a lakefront setting, and any number of activities in the casino, conference center, retail village, and spa.

STATS
349 guestrooms, including 35 suites;
3 restaurants and lounges;
357,000-square-foot site

FEATURES
30,000-square-foot Ritz-Carlton Spa®, Lake Las Vegas; fitness center/health club; conference facility with a 12,000-square-foot ballroom; business center; private white-sand beach; water sports; pool and whirlpool; two 18-hole golf courses and golf clubhouses; retail village; casino; marina and private yachts, water taxis

KUDOS
One of the Best Spas in North America by Condé Nast Traveler
America's 10 Best New Public Courses by Golf Digest

DON'T MISS
The many outdoor amenities available for all activity and fitness levels: from relaxing gondola rides, yacht tours, stargazing and flights over the Grand Canyon, to kayaking, hiking, fly fishing, extreme mountain biking, and white water rafting

GUESTS SAY
"This is a truly elegant property that does not need glitter to succeed; the resort gives a different spin to the Las Vegas experience."

A three-story bridge structure, emulating Italy's Ponte Vecchio, spans the resort's 320-acre lake, which can be seen from all guestrooms in The Ritz-Carlton, Lake Las Vegas. The rooms are decorated in a warm palette with imported furnishings and also offer sweeping views of the nearby mountains.

Visitors to the two-story spa can partake of desert- and Tuscan-inspired treatments in pavilions surrounding an interior Italian garden courtyard. The casino and conference center attached to the hotel overlook the retail village as well as the formal gardens and lake. A wall of windows also enables diners at The Medici Café and Terrace to enjoy the views. Two award-winning championship golf courses are situated alongside the natural splendor of the desert floor.

The neighboring MonteLago Village has additional accommodations including studio, one-, two-, and three-bedroom luxury condominium units, many available through the hotel reservation system. Cobblestone streets meander through the village, leading to 25 retail, dining, and entertainment venues.

Newport Coast, California, USA

MARRIOTT'S NEWPORT COAST VILLAS

Perched high upon a bluff overlooking the Pacific Ocean, this vacation ownership resort offers sweeping views of the Southern California coastline.

STATS
461 guestrooms; 75-acre site

FEATURES
Spa Pacifica; fitness center with sauna and steam room; business center in owner's lounge; 3 heated pools, 5 outdoor whirlpool spas; The Marketplace; town plaza; reception building; sales center; games room

KUDOS
"ACE Project of Excellence," Gold Award by the American Resort Development Association (ARDA) ARDY Gold Awards
"Site Design and Utilization," Gold Award by the American Resort Development Association (ARDA) ARDY Gold Awards
Recognized for "Most Creative Vacation Architecture" by Marriott Vacation Club International

DON'T MISS
Spa Pacifica, with its 6 indoor treatment rooms and 2 outdoor cabanas

GUESTS SAY
"We loved the at-home feel of this resort. The suites are huge, the landscaping is beautiful, and the view is worth a million dollars."

The resort's design evokes both the warmth of a traditional Tuscan hillside village and the opulent style of Newport Beach. At the heart of the property and entrance to the villas is a Mediterranean-inspired town plaza, complete with tower and 16-foot-tall hand-chiseled fountain of Poseidon, the Greek god of the sea.

The main registration building features mosaic ceramic tile, decorative woodwork, sculpted plaster detailing, and Spanish clay tile roofs. Elegantly appointed and spacious two-bedroom villas accommodate up to eight guests in low-rise buildings that are oriented to maximize views of the canyon and coastline from private balconies.

There are many attractions outside of the resort—for example, the Pelican Hill Golf Club, Crystal Cove State Park, and Newport Beach Harbor—as well as on the property, where guests can swim in one of the three outdoor pools, shop and dine at The Piazza, or simply relax in the spa.

New Orleans, Louisiana, USA

MASQUERADE AT HARRAH'S

This one-of-a-kind, ultra-modern casino, performance, and entertainment venue in the heart of Harrah's casino has become the "must-see" attraction for locals and visitors in New Orleans.

Designed in a "Masquerade" New Orleans baroque style, this gathering space is anchored by a sleek, four-story video tower with a 360-degree stage wrapped around its core that serves as the centerpiece of the destination. Merging art and technology, the tower creates an ever-changing multi-sensory experience incorporating audio, video, intelligent lighting, and special effects including faux-fire. Circling the tower's base is the Ice Bar, a 32-foot bar topped with solid ice, where the trend-seekers go for live entertainment, go-go dancers, and drink specials served by performers called bevertainers.

A 53-foot ceiling displays a night sky-themed mural and fiber optic galaxy that gives the space a dramatic outdoor feel. Completing the experience is an intimate private lounge, dance floor, a stage for live shows, table games, and slots.

South Pender Island, British Columbia, Canada

POETS COVE RESORT & SPA

A favorite port of call for leisure boaters and travelers, guests can take a water taxi from Sidney (on Vancouver Island) to Bedwell Harbour or approach the island by ferry.

The resort, with a 22-room lodge and a cluster of seaside cottages and villas, was designed with a contemporary Pacific-Northwest look and a plush but informal ambience. All the accommodations capture ocean or forest-and-water views and feature fireplaces and luxurious bathtubs. Cottages and villas have two or three bedrooms, gourmet kitchens, decks, and outdoor hot tubs.

Adventurous guests can go kayaking, sailing, cycling, or hiking in the breathtaking scenery for which the area is known. Other, more placid activities include dining on fresh Pacific-Northwest cuisine, or partaking of any one of the locally inspired treatments at the resort's Susurrus Spa. Outside the spa, guests can discover a sandstone steam cave beneath a waterfall and an ocean-view hot tub at the waterfall's base.

Orlando, Florida, USA

PORTOFINO BAY HOTEL AT UNIVERSAL ORLANDO®, A LOEWS HOTEL

Nestled in a picturesque bay, this luxurious hotel recreates the charm and romance of the sunny seaside village of Portofino, Italy, right down to the cobblestone streets, sun-washed stucco façades, and outdoor cafés.

STATS
750 guestrooms and suites; 7 restaurants and lounges; 18.7-acre site

FEATURES
2,300-square-foot Mandara Spa, including a health and fitness facility and salon; 42,000 square feet of convention/function/meeting space, including a 15,000-square-foot ballroom; business center; 3 themed swimming pools, including a villa pool with private cabanas and a large beach pool with Roman aqueduct-styled water slide; retail boutique; bocce ball court; Campo Portofino

KUDOS
Connoisseur's Choice Award
by *Resorts & Great Hotels*

Top 20 Most Family-Friendly Resorts in the U.S. and Canada
by *Travel+Leisure Family Magazine*

World's Top (on-site) Theme Park Hotel
by *Theme Park Insider*

DON'T MISS
Taking the water taxi directly to the Universal attractions and using your room key as a fast pass to avoid the lines

GUESTS SAY
"Portofino is themed so well, you really get that laid-back feel of a charming part of Italy in the middle of Orlando! It really is La Dolce Vita ... plus some!"

The primary design objective was to re-interpret the romantic village town of Portofino, on the Italian Riviera, and provide the superior guest amenities and services desired for Universal's first destination resort hotel.

The design team, which spent several months in Italy doing research, recreated this historic village by faithfully replicating the perimeter of the harbor, with the guestrooms and restaurants encircling the waterfront identically to the layout of the original village. A series of rivers and canals connects the hotel to Universal's entertainment attractions, including Universal Studios, City Walk, and Islands of Adventure theme park. Upon arrival at the porte-cochère, a classical fountain greets guests, and the lobby offers fantastic views of the harbor.

Hollywood, California, USA

RENAISSANCE HOLLYWOOD HOTEL & SPA

Boasting a sophisticated, modern design and breathtaking views of Los Angeles, this dazzling landmark hotel captures the energy of today's Hollywood.

STATS
637 guestrooms and suites; restaurant and bar; 8-acre site

FEATURES
SPA LUCE, fitness center; 65,000 square feet of meeting space; business center; rooftop outdoor pool; private cabanas on pool terrace; gift shop; adjoining entertainment center with retail shops, restaurants, and theaters

KUDOS
Hotel of the Year by Renaissance Hotels and Resorts

DON'T MISS
The Kodak Theatre, Grauman's Chinese Theatre, as well as Hollywood and Highland shopping/entertainment complex, all immediately accessible from the hotel

GUESTS SAY
"The Renaissance is hip and happening and abounds in amazing modern art everywhere!"

The newly renovated and upgraded hotel—converted from what was formerly a Holiday Inn—has sparked a dramatic rebirth of Hollywood Boulevard and has been operating at maximum capacity since opening.

More than 70 original works of art were assembled or commissioned for their affinity to the hotel's design and its cultural sense of place. Many of the suites and executive guestrooms provide space for small business meetings and exhilarating views of Los Angeles and the Hollywood Hills.

A 3,500-square-foot Panorama Suite offers floor-to-ceiling windows with mesmerizing, 270-degree vistas, a baby grand piano, and an oversized Jacuzzi in the master bathroom. A roof-top pool terrace rises 70 feet above Hollywood Boulevard where, at street level, guests can immediately access the Kodak Theatre and a vast array of entertainment and shopping options. Twist, the hotel's ultra-stylish dining venue, is located on the mezzanine level.

Phoenix, Arizona, USA

SHERATON WILD HORSE PASS RESORT & SPA

The Gila River Indian Community, which represents the Pima and Maricopa tribal cultures, wanted a resort that would find its design roots in their history and also respect the natural environment.

Without succumbing to the fantasy or caricature that characterizes many contemporary themed resorts, the design process began with the development of a heritage story and an authentic cultural program. The resort's traditional architectural forms include *vahtos* (trellis-like shade-providing structures) and a *humapek ke'* (gathering place). A 2.5-mile river feature is incorporated throughout the entire development, linking the various components and echoing the tribes' reverence for the Gila River.

The resort is located in the Sonoran Desert on an expanse of rugged Arizona landscape where the ancient vistas, mountains, and roaming wild horses remain untouched. The architecture, design, art, and legends of the Pima and Maricopa tribes are celebrated in every detail imaginable—indoors and out—in this destination resort.

Palm Desert, California, USA

SPA DESERT SPRINGS

A waterfall at check-in immediately puts guests into a relaxation mode, and the landscaped indoor–outdoor spaces serve as sanctuaries for the body, mind, and spirit.

STATS
33,000-square-foot spa; 4,000-square-foot fitness center; yoga studio

FEATURES
22 state-of-the-art Body Master stations; walking and jogging paths; changing facilities; lap pool; steam room; therapy baths; full-service beauty salon

DON'T MISS
Warm oil gently poured over your "third eye"

GUESTS SAY
"The spa was beautifully appointed. The lounges (both the female and coed) are comfortable and give you a great place to relax and unwind before any treatment."

All 47 treatment rooms in the Spa Desert Springs at Desert Springs JW Marriott Resort & Spa feature natural materials, the latest in spa technology, and uniquely luxurious environments. There is a 600-square-foot private suite—the Spa Sanctuary—with an exclusive entrance, two-person hydrotherapy tub in a walled-in private courtyard, and another tub indoors. Sanctuary guests can enjoy a programmable shower and their own living area with a fireplace and high-definition TV. A separate suite designed for couples includes private treatment rooms and another hydrotherapy tub. The "spa within a spa" allows small groups to relax in a suite with its own lounge and treatment rooms—perfect for bridal parties, getaways, and romantic relaxation.

In addition to enjoying the *hammams* (Turkish steam chambers infused with essential oils), guests can also relax in large soaking whirlpools and window-wrapped saunas overlooking the resort's golf course. The digitally programmable showers offer seven types of shower heads. A Spa Bistro delivers healthy fare from its perch overlooking the pool and mountain vistas, and there is also a full spa retail shop and separate hair, manicure, and pedicure salons. The Spa Desert Springs is part of a luxury resort that sits on 450 acres of lush, landscaped grounds and lagoons with the dramatic backdrop of three mountain ranges.

Palm Beach, Florida, USA

THE BREAKERS PALM BEACH

Now in its second century, The Breakers retains its famed status as a luxury beachfront resort by adapting to the needs of future generations.

STATS
550 guestrooms, including 58 suites; 9 restaurants; 140 oceanfront acres

FEATURES
20,000-square-foot, oceanfront Spa and Beach Club; 2 fitness centers; Oceanfront Conference Center, including 58,000 square feet of meeting space; 24/7 business center; watersport center; grand cabanas with concierge; beach bungalows on private beach; 10 tennis courts; 5 pools; 4 whirlpool spas; two 18-hole championship golf courses; golf clubhouse; 12 shopping boutiques; Family Entertainment Center; Flagler Club; private residences

KUDOS
Top 50 Resorts in the United States by *Condé Nast Traveler*
100 Best Places to Stay by *Robb Report*
#1 Family-Friendly Resort in the U.S. by *Child*

DON'T MISS
The peaceful ambience of the adults-only relaxation pool.

GUESTS SAY
"Wonderful detailing throughout; the resort exudes a placid atmosphere of relaxed luxury."

The Italian Renaissance-style hotel keeps expanding to meet the most contemporary expectations for a completely self-contained luxury destination. The Oceanfront Conference Center, Spa and Beach Club, new golf clubhouse, and even the redesigned front drive reflect the qualities that have long drawn guests back to The Breakers—a truly timeless, elegant and relevant resort.

A landscaped drive leads to a Florentine fountain, patterned after the one at the Boboli Gardens in Florence, and sets the tone for this stately manor. Listed on the National Register of Historic Places, the resort combines the elegant comforts of a grand residence with the energized amenities of a sophisticated family resort.

Newport Beach, California, USA

THE ISLAND HOTEL

The design challenge for this property, formerly the Four Seasons Hotel Newport Beach, was to create a resort environment on a tight urban site.

STATS
295 guestrooms, including 83 suites;
2 restaurants; 4.5-acre site

FEATURES
4,000-square-foot spa; fitness center; 30,000
square feet of meeting and function space,
including two ballrooms and 10 meeting
rooms; business center; 2 tennis courts;
3,000-square-foot pool

KUDOS
Five Diamonds
by *Automobile Association of America*
Member of The Leading Hotels of the World
Best Hotels in the Continental
United States and Canada
by *Travel+Leisure*

DON'T MISS
The fireplace by the pool—a great place to
unwind with a drink in the evening or a
paper in the morning

GUESTS SAY
"The hotel is lovely and the pool area is quite
relaxing. We especially liked the huge whirlpool
with the fountain in the middle."

The architects angled a 19-story stepped-back tower to provide guests with panoramic views of the Pacific Ocean and Newport Harbor, yet still allowed space for a large outdoor pool, tennis courts, terraces, and park-like landscaping.

A cantilevered porte-cochère offers guests an immediate sense of spaciousness. Several design features—the tower's chamfered edges, the softening effect of landscaped niches at each of the building's elevations, terraced balconies, and the private driveway entry and spacious turn-around—contribute to the experience of the hotel as a secluded retreat.

Pasadena, California, USA

THE LANGHAM, HUNTINGTON HOTEL & SPA

Set in the San Gabriel Mountain foothills of Pasadena, this grand hotel—originally built in 1907 as a mecca for winter sojourners—has been revitalized as a world-class luxury resort.

The architects went to great lengths to preserve the hotel's heritage, rebuilding and recycling wherever possible to lend new vitality to this historic landmark. An entry portal, recalling the original archway used for horse carriages, was reproduced to create a new entryway and lobby.

Once used as a dining room, The Viennese Ballroom was renamed for the beautiful chandeliers made for the hotel in Vienna in the early 1930s. The Georgian Room's arched ceiling features original stained-glass windows discovered during the restoration.

Several cottages on the property were restored for guest use: one, an English-style 1930s bungalow, has become the hotel's health club; the Clara Vista Cottage executive and leisure retreat is now a completely restored mansion.

Las Vegas, Nevada, USA

THE MANSION AT MGM GRAND

Capturing the elegance and the exclusivity of an Italian palazzo, the Mansion caters to the invited guests of the MGM Grand Casino.

STATS
29 villas; private restaurant and wine room;
5.35-acre site

FEATURES
Spa; Great Hall and Grand Salon for meetings/
events; indoor and outdoor pools; formal gardens
with fountains, reflecting pools, and
handcrafted sculptures

KUDOS
Best of the Best by *Robb Report*

DON'T MISS
Swimming in your own luxurious private pool

GUESTS SAY
"The Mansion may be the finest place in the
world to stay."

Guests are chauffeured through a private gate that leads to a granite cobblestone-paved courtyard featuring a magnificent limestone fountain designed by the architects and hand-carved by master craftsmen in Italy. The design goal was to transport guests to another place, specifically, the Italian Tuscan region.

The grand structure includes 21 atrium villas and eight garden villas, which range in size from 2,600 to 13,000 square feet. Some of the villas have libraries and indoor pools, and all contain carved limestone mantles, dining rooms, and original artwork. The largest villas also include exercise and media rooms as well as additional bedrooms.

All of the exquisite atrium villas overlook the central atrium garden with its fountains and reflecting pools, and formal Italian gardens also frame the spa, restaurant, and meeting spaces. To ensure the greatest level of privacy and security, the hotel is laid out so that guests can get to any room and to the casino through an enclosed climate-controlled atrium, without going outside.

Las Vegas, Nevada, USA

THE PALACE TOWER AT CAESARS PALACE

The first themed hotel and casino in Las Vegas is still delighting tourists with its trademark Roman architecture style.

STATS
1,134 guestrooms and suites;
12 restaurants/lounges in Palace Tower;
86-acre site

FEATURES
22,000-square-foot Qua Baths & Spa; fitness center; 110,000 square feet of banquet and meeting facilities; 3 tennis courts; 4.5-acre swimming complex; 15,000 square feet of added retail; 8,200 square feet of added casino

KUDOS
Best Hotels in the Continental United States and Canada by *Travel+Leisure*

DON'T MISS
The lavish Garden of the Gods pool oasis—a complex of Roman-style gardens, baths, and fitness areas anchored by the Neptune lap pool

GUESTS SAY
"The hotel itself is beautiful and the rooms are luxurious; there are lots of fountains and statues throughout and the pool areas are really something special."

A 29-story tower was designed to align with the resort's theme, using exterior fluted columns and Corinthian capitals and pediments. Following the line of the Greco-Roman façade, Palace Tower guestrooms vary in size from 500 to 750 square feet, each with a sitting area and 9-foot ceilings to enhance the feeling of spaciousness.

Two of the Tower's upper floors house 30 luxury suites, and two of the lower floors are devoted to banquet and meeting facilities, reflecting an influx of high-end corporate travelers to the Las Vegas tourist market. A 30,000-square-foot ballroom with 21-foot-high ceilings accommodates technical support for headliner entertainment.

The Tower's second floor includes a full-service spa and fitness center. An elaborate Garden of the Gods swimming complex includes four marble-lined swimming pools and two whirlpools, three tennis courts, plus landscaped gardens, statuary, and fountains.

Dana Point, California, USA

THE RITZ-CARLTON, LAGUNA NIGUEL

Situated on a 150-foot-high bluff overlooking the Pacific Ocean, this resort blends unobtrusively with its setting while offering guests magnificent views of Santa Catalina Island and an unparalleled sense of privacy and exclusivity.

The understated colors and materials used in the resort's design blend with the natural setting, giving the resort the appearance of a Spanish Mediterranean-style village, typical of the Mission period of Southern California. By situating the first floor 15 feet below the existing grade, the building appears to be melded to the bluff.

Architects used the ocean as the focal point and designed the resort in two L-shaped wings to extend the sense of seclusion from inside the hotel, while providing discreet public access to the beach below for residents.

Guestrooms offer all the technological amenities guests want today, while the use of fine marbles, specially woven carpets, and richly detailed wood paneling exudes an atmosphere of luxury and comfort. Guests can enjoy the dramatic cliffside views from the resort's dining, library, fitness, and spa facilities.

Naples, Florida, USA

THE RITZ-CARLTON, NAPLES

This palatial and timeless resort takes full advantage of its prime beachfront location and is often credited with ushering in a new era of tourism on Florida's Paradise Coast.

The classic turn-of-the-century symmetry and Mediterranean design, together with courtyards, stone fountains, and manicured gardens, delight guests with unexpected vistas at every turn. The hotel's twin belvedere towers, gracefully arched windows, and classic balustrades are carefully reminiscent of the monumental villas of Italy and late-nineteenth-century hotels of Florida. Off the two-level lobby, a grand staircase climbs to the mezzanine and its ballrooms.

The building's U-shape provides every guestroom with an ocean view, some directly overlooking the mangroves and the beach. The resort was designed to suit the Florida climate, with windows sheltered under protective arcades or shaded by balconies. All habitable spaces are at least 13 feet above the natural grade for flood control, and the resort has careful systems in place to protect the delicate ecosystem of wetlands that surround it.

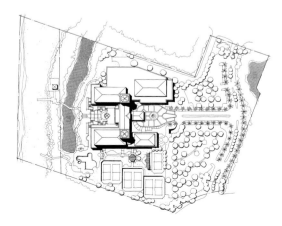

Las Vegas, Nevada, USA

THE VENETIAN RESORT-HOTEL-CASINO

Authenticity is the basis for fantasy in this Venice-themed resort hotel and casino located in the heart of the glittery Las Vegas strip.

STATS
3,036 suites on 35 floors; 11 restaurants; 63-acre site (phase one)

FEATURES
Canyon Ranch Spa Club; fitness center; 1.9 million square feet of meeting, convention, and trade show space; business center; 11-acre rooftop pool deck and Italian gardens; 500,000 square feet of retail/entertainment; 120,000-square-foot casino; 4-level performance center

KUDOS
Gold Medallion Design Award by *Casino Executive*
Best Overall Casino Hotel by *Casino Player*
Award of Excellence by Urban Land Institute

DON'T MISS
The Grand Canal Shoppes and gondola ride along a recreated Venice cityscape

GUESTS SAY
"My favorite place to stay in Vegas; you can't beat the huge suites and sheer opulence."

Architects worked alongside historians to recreate the feeling of being transported to 15th-century Venice, complete with exact replicas of the Doge's Palace, St Mark's Square, the Rialto Bridge, the Ca D'Oro, and the Campanile Tower, as well as hand-painted frescoes, canals, and gondolas.

The resort is designed as a complete destination for every type of visitor, enabling families, honeymooners, conventioneers, gamers, and gourmands to experience the wonder of Renaissance Italy—without ever leaving the resort grounds.

All of the 700-square-foot suites feature marble foyers, oversized bathrooms, and sunken living rooms, and are designed to provide a peaceful respite from the action.

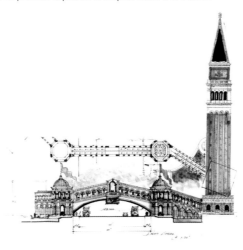

NEW DESTINATIONS

ALMAZA SPA HOTEL

Alexandria, Egypt

The architectural vision for this 250-room, five-star hotel and spa is a contemporary campus comprising one- to three-story structures constructed from a combination of modern and vernacular materials. Local stone provides a thermal mass, which retains heat during the day and radiates it back on cool nights, and the buildings are designed to take advantage of solar shading. Located on the Mediterranean coast, and developed by Travco Group International, the hotel includes a series of landscaped courtyards and pools terracing down towards the bay.

BARDESSONO INN AND SPA

Yountville, California, USA

A 62-room boutique luxury lodge in the heart of Napa Valley, this environmentally friendly inn includes a spa, a 75-foot-long rooftop infinity pool, a fine dining restaurant, and generous meeting space. The design reflects a blending of Napa's agrarian character with the high refinement of its fine wines. Incorporating solar and geothermal energy, sophisticated energy-management systems, sustainable building materials, and organic landscape management practices, the project is pursuing a LEED Gold Certification.

CONGHUA HOT SPRINGS RESORT

Guangzhou, China

A five-star golf resort and conference center, this hotel is located on a 35-acre site that is part of a larger master plan of resort properties adjacent to the Liuxi River. In addition to the 180-room hotel, Conghua Hot Springs Resort includes a luxury spa, a conference center, a ballroom, and a video center as well as a golf clubhouse. As part of the resort's sustainable design, each building includes a unique photovoltaic system integrated into the roofing system.

FIJI NAVILACA RESORT & SPA

Vanua Levu Island, Fiji

Guests enter this tropical resort via a meandering road through a forest of giant rain trees dripping with bromeliads. High-pitched thatched roofs in Fijian *bure* style come into view and an open-air lobby greets visitors with dramatic ocean views. Each of the one- and two-bedroom villas includes an outdoor shower, plunge pool, and bathtub next to a garden-view glass wall. Guests can also enjoy beachside restaurants, bars, pools, outdoor spa treatment *bures*, a fitness center, and water activities at the marina.

FOUR SEASONS RESORT HAINAN AT SHENZHOU

Hainan, China

This luxury villa resort is nestled within a lush tropical valley with views of the South China Sea. In order to preserve its natural beauty, the site is entered through a tunnel beneath the western headland. The 58 hotel villas and 30 residences are contemporary in design with open floor plans and individual private pools. From the main arrival pavilion, guests take the inclinator lift up 260 feet to the spa and specialty restaurant; both have spectacular 270-degree views.

FOUR SEASONS RESORT MAURITIUS AT ANAHITA

Beau Champ, Mauritius

Cocooned within a private sanctuary, Four Seasons Resort Mauritius provides guests with amazing views of crystal-blue waters and green-blanketed mountains. The resort community includes a five-star hotel, luxury villas, a specialty restaurant, an Ernie Els 18-hole golf course with clubhouse, a beach club, a health spa with treatment pavilions, and a boardwalk over the water and through a mangrove-tree forest. Leisure activities available on the 432-acre site include dining, shopping, and recreation as well as ecological interaction and education programs.

GRAND HYATT KUALA LUMPUR

Kuala Lumpur, Malaysia

When guests first arrive at this 40-story, five-star hotel, they ride express lifts to the sky lobby on the very top floor where breathtaking, 360-degree views of downtown Kuala Lumpur greet them. In addition to the hotel's 357 guestrooms on floors 21 through 37, this mixed-use development high-rise also includes serviced apartments and offices. The project is centrally located adjacent to the famous Petronas Twin Towers and the Kuala Lumpur Convention Centre.

HOTEL MONTE MULINI

Istria, Croatia

Located in an historic coastal city along the Adriatic coast, this year-round hotel features 120 rooms including 19 luxury suites—along with activities and ambiences suitable for each season. With a nature reserve located just across the bay and the main promenade of the city of Rovinj at its feet, the hotel's décor integrates both urban and natural elements. Sustainable features include extended roof overhangs for solar shading and the use of natural building materials such as locally quarried stone.

NEW DESTINATIONS

HOTEL PREKO

Ugljan, Croatia

This 60-room luxury boutique hotel is situated directly in front of the old harbor in the historic island town of Preko. The ancient fishing village's urban center in which the hotel is located also includes a promenade as well as Mediterranean-style restaurants and taverns. Located along the Adriatic coast, Preko was once a favored summer residential community for noble families from nearby Zadar. The island's bays are ideal for diving, and the inland terrain is suitable for trekking, bicycling, and exploring.

LA PUNTA PAPAGAYO

Guanacaste, Costa Rica

This 60-acre, five-star resort development in Costa Rica comprises a luxury hotel and spa, private villas and estate homes, as well as an artisan and retail village. Designed with a blend of sophisticated elegance and relaxed comfort, the resort is set between verdant forests and pristine waters, and incorporates the artful use of natural materials. La Punta Papagayo is located in the northwest region of the country's Guanacaste province, overlooking the Gulf of Papagayo and the Bay of Colebra.

MOHEGAN SUN'S PROJECT HORIZON

Uncasville, Connecticut, USA

Project Horizon was created in response to the popularity of this New England hot spot, which welcomes 35,000 daily visitors for gaming, dining, shopping, and entertainment. The new portion of the property includes a 64,000-square-foot Casino of the Wind and a 919-room hotel featuring 261 rooms that have a House of Blues® theme. There is also a House of Blues® Music Hall and a members-only Foundation Room. The additional 115,000 square feet encompass retail and restaurant space as well as a spa and meeting/function rooms.

OCEAN SILK ROAD PALACE

Quanzhou, China

For this first hotel in Ocean City Resort, the design was inspired by events occurring over 750 years ago—the decline of the Silk Road and the rise of ocean-going trade that positioned Quanzhou as the region's main port. Given its global trading history, the area is known for its cultural diversity. The Silk Road story is told in friezes and frescos throughout this luxury hotel property, which includes 400 guestrooms and suites, a conference center, entertainment complex, spa, outdoor pools, and gardens.

OCEAN VILLAGE MARINA

Southampton, United Kingdom

Sustainability is a key goal for this mixed-use waterfront development that includes a 15-story, 225-guestroom, five-star hotel on the marina in Southampton. For example, the innovative use of a low-temperature seawater system to chill guestrooms results in lower carbon emissions than conventional air conditioning. A spacious two-story lobby welcomes hotel visitors and offers them a restaurant, café, bar, and spa as well as conference facilities for 700 guests.

PARK HYATT ALMATY

Almaty, Kazakhstan

Situated opposite the Almaty Opera House, the Park Hyatt is a city-center hotel with 150 guestrooms and 40 serviced apartments. The hotel's columnar façade and grand arcade reflect the classical styling of historic buildings in the downtown area. With its restaurants and retail shops, the property's arcade creates an activity hub that attracts hotel guests and city residents. The Park Hyatt's stately design features columns, balconies and tall arched windows on the exterior as well as chandeliers and distinctive décor throughout the interior.

PLAYA PELICANO

Playa Pelicano, Costa Rica

Along with the 55,000-square-foot spa, wellness, and fitness center, the Playa Pelicano destination spa resort includes a beach club and activity center, hotel guestrooms, condo/hotel units, and *casitas* (villas). All are tucked among the trees and blended with the environment through careful use of natural materials such as stone and wood, with colors similar to those found in the forests of Costa Rica. Roof overhangs, wall placements, and open-air rooms provide shade and cool breezes to enhance the tropical experience while affording comfort and luxury for guests and residents.

PUERTAS AL CIELO

Puerto Los Cabos, Mexico

At the heart of the resort are the individual *casa* suites—embracing private courtyard gardens, individual plunge pools, hand-cut fieldstone-walled outdoor showers, freestanding soaking tubs, and shaded terraces—all with high-vaulted *palapa*-roofed ceilings and views of the Pacific Ocean. Open patios with fountains, trellises providing geometrical shade patterns, and built-in seating areas are tactile elements of the resort's Mexican-inspired architecture. The contemporary design of this retreat, its luxurious décor, and its rooftop pool epitomize the name *Puertas al Cielo*, which means "Doorway to Heaven."

NEW DESTINATIONS

REGENT HOTEL BANGKOK

SHAZA HOTEL AND RESIDENCES

SHERATON XIXI

THE RITZ-CARLTON, BANGALORE

Bangkok, Thailand

This five-star urban hotel marries design elements that are distinctly Thai with embellishments of retro-1950s style in an imaginative combination that suits international tastes and contemporary expectations. The 30-story hotel has 327 guestrooms, an executive lounge and suite, four restaurants with a wine bar and a whiskey bar, function and meeting rooms, a ballroom, a spa with 14 treatment rooms, a salon, and an indoor swimming pool. The accompanying 40-story tower includes 350 condominium units.

Cairo, Egypt

Located in downtown Cairo, this landmark tower is a contemporary urban oasis that provides guests with the highest international standards of service and the purest tradition of Middle Eastern hospitality. The three-story, glass-enclosed sky-lobby—perched 50 floors above the edge of the Nile River—offers stunning views of the capital city and the enduring Pyramids. The 650-foot-tall hotel includes 350 guestrooms and 78 luxury apartments. This is one of the first properties in Kempinski Hotels' new Shaza brand.

Hangzhou, China

The design for this five-star resort hotel—with its 380 guestrooms, spa and fitness club, indoor pool, and conference center—is based on the circle: a perfect geometric shape, the universal symbol of unity. The architects also drew inspiration from the Chinese proverb, "Flowers are beautiful when the moon is full." The foliage, courtyards, pools, waterfall, and canal are interconnected by walkways, providing a lovely stroll by day or by moonlight. One fine dining option features private gazebos, resembling pagodas, along the picturesque canal.

Bangalore, India

This 16-story, five-star hotel encompasses 267 guestrooms including 27 suites, conference facilities, a luxury spa, fitness center, specialty retail shops, four restaurants, a club lounge, and a rooftop terrace. All are designed to reflect contemporary Indian influences. Due to the restrictive nature of the terrain, the architects created an innovative "footprint" for the hotel: the L-shaped structure includes a long-thin leg and a shorter, fatter "foot" that allows for maximum use of the site.

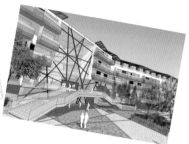

SENTOSA QUAYSIDE COLLECTION

Singapore

With downtown Singapore nearby, this contemporary community—on a peninsula with yachts moored on two sides—merges marina activities, striking architectural forms, and a network of promenades, waterways, and fountains. The private residences focus on spectacular waterway views and maximize the pleasures of a waterfront lifestyle. A gracefully arcing shell-shaped roof hovers lightly above rooftop garden terraces on the retail and entertainment center, while the six-story hotel anchors the peninsula with a gentle bend that cups the pool and gardens at the edge of the land.

TRUMP AT CAP CANA

Dominican Republic

The five-star Trump at Cap Cana hotel and condominium project is located on nearly 30 acres of lush landscape and a natural white-sand beach. The property has more than 300 guestrooms, a 25,000-square-foot spa including treatment rooms floating above the water, and 15,000 square feet of meeting space. The architecture is a contemporary interpretation of island design, using clean lines and details in conjunction with natural, indigenous materials to create an upscale destination that remains sensitive to the surrounding environment.

VALE DO LOBO

Algarve, Portugal

This new five-star hotel, designed to be the flagship structure for the resort, includes 159 guestrooms and 43 luxury serviced apartments. The dramatically sculptured building takes its shape and color from the famous sandy cliffs of the Algarve. The playful nature of the façade continues into the hotel's courtyard and guestroom balconies, where changing shapes afford stunning views of landscaped pool courtyards and fairways. A suspended glass box between the executive meeting center and the hotel overlooks the 9th hole from the hotel's Sky Bar.

VICEROY ANGUILLA RESORT AND RESIDENCES

Anguilla, British West Indies

The contemporary design for Viceroy Anguilla blends Caribbean warmth with sophisticated luxury. One- and two-bedroom bluff-top resort residences are located at the property's center, offering sweeping views of the bay's white-sand beaches. Low-rise beachfront resort residences showcase the stunning views of Meads Bay. Additional freestanding villas on the 27-acre site overlook Barnes Bay and the ocean. Ocean water activities are naturally in abundance as are opportunities for simply relaxing and enjoying the scenery.

PROJECT DATA

Interior Designer: WATG
Photography: Courtesy Conrad Maldives Rangali Island

Denia Marriott La Sella Golf Resort & Spa 116
Denia, Alicante, Spain
Client/Owner: Promociones Denia S.L.
Architect: WATG
Associate Architect: Ingenieria Diez Cisneros (IDC); Poole and Poole Arquitectos
Landscape Architect: Hyland Edgar Driver
Interior Designer: WATG
Contractor: Brown and Root; Ingenieria Diez Cisneros (IDC)
Photography: Courtesy Marriott International

Disney's Grand Floridian Resort & Spa 256
Walt Disney World® Resort, Lake Buena Vista, Florida, USA
Client/Owner: Disney Development Company
Architect: WATG
Associate Architect: Walt Disney Imagineering
Landscape Architect: Peridian Group
Interior Designer: Intradesign
Contractor: Frank J. Rooney, Inc.
Photography: Copyright Disney Enterprises, Inc.

Disneyland® Hotel 118
The Disneyland® Resort Paris, Paris, France
Client/Owner: Euro Disney SCA (Euro Disneyland Corporation)
Architect: WATG
Associate Architect: Richard Martinet Architects (Walt Disney Imagineering)
Landscape Architect: POD/Sasaki; EDAW; Michael Massot
Interior Designer: JMI Design Inc.; Pierre-Yves Rochon S.A.
Contractor: Bovis International Ltd.
Photography: Copyright Disney Enterprises, Inc.

Emirates Hills Villa Estates 198
Dubai, United Arab Emirates
Client/Owner: EMAAR PROPERTIES
Architect: WATG
Associate Architect: Rice Perry Ellis
Landscape Architect: The Collaborative West; Al Khatib Cracknell
Interior Designer: Design Line Interiors; Logam Designs
Golf Course Architect: Colin Montgomerie; Desmond Muirhead Inc.
Contractor: Al Naboodah Laing; Arabtec
Photography: Courtesy Emirates Hills

Emirates Palace 200
Abu Dhabi, United Arab Emirates
Client/Owner: The Government of Abu Dhabi's Executive Committee Ministry of Protocol;
Turner International (Project Manager)
Architect: WATG
Associate Architect: WATG/KEO Alliance; Abu Dhabi, UAE
Landscape Architect: Derek Lovejoy Partnership, London
Interior Designer: KY&A Associates, Inc., Abu Dhabi
Contractor: RSEA
Photography: Courtesy Emirates Palace

Fairmont Towers Heliopolis 204
Heliopolis, Cairo, Egypt
Client/Owner: Gulf Egypt for Hotels & Tourism
Architect: WATG
Landscape Architect: WATG
Interior Designer: WATG
Contractor: CCC
Photography: Anthony Parkinson

Four Seasons Golf Club Dubai Festival City 208
Dubai, United Arab Emirates
Client/Owner: Dubai Festival City
Architect: WATG
Golf Course Architect: Robert Trent Jones II
Interior Designer: Yabu Pushelberg
Photography: Paul Thuysbaert; Courtesy Four Seasons Golf Club Dubai Festival City

Four Seasons Hotel Bangkok 22
Bangkok, Thailand
Client/Owner: The Rajdamri Hotel Public Company Ltd.
Architect: WATG
Associate Architect: Dan Wongprasat
Landscape Architect: Khun Sithiporn Thonavanik
Interior Designer: Rifenberg/Rirkrit
Contractor: Kay Thai Construction Ltd.
Photography: Robert McLeod; Courtesy Four Seasons Hotels & Resorts

Four Seasons Hotel Dublin 120
Dublin, Ireland
Client/Owner: Nollaig Nominee Ltd.; Simmonscourt Holdings Ltd.
Architect: WATG
Associate Architect: Michael Collins Associates
Landscape Architect: Derek Lovejoy Partnership; SAP Landscapes
Interior Designer: Frank Nicholson Inc.
Contractor: G&T Crampton Ltd.
Photography: Jaime Ardiles-Arce; Andrew Bradley

Four Seasons Hotel Mexico, D.F. 188
Mexico City, Mexico
Client/Owner: Proparmex S.A. de C.V.
Architect: WATG
Associate Architect: Sergio Alvarez; Aleman / GTM International
Interior Designer: Inter Art
Contractor: Huartym S.A. de C.V.
Photography: Peter Vitale; Courtesy Four Seasons Hotels & Resorts

Four Seasons Hotel Tokyo at Chinzan-so 26
Tokyo, Japan
Client/Owner: Fujita Tourist Enterprises Co. Ltd.
Architect: WATG
Associate Architect: Yozo Shibata & Associates Architects & Designers
Landscape Architect: The Dike Partnership
Interior Designer: Frank Nicholson, Inc.
Contractor: Shimizu Construction Company, Ltd.
Photography: Gensho Haga; Courtesy Four Seasons Hotels & Resorts

Four Seasons Hotel Westlake Village 258
Westlake Village, California, USA
Client/ Owner: David H. Murdock; Westlake Wellbeing Properties LLC
Architect: WATG; Arnold C. Savrann
Landscape Architect: David H. Murdock; L. Newman Design Group, Inc.
Interior Designer: WATG; Arnold C. Savrann
Contractor: Matt Construction
Photography: Barbara Kraft; David Lena; Peter Vitale

Four Seasons Resort Aviara 264
Carlsbad, California, USA
Client/Owner: Aviara Resort Associates Limited Partnership
Architect: WATG
Landscape Architect: IVY Landscape Architects; ONA Landscape
Golf Course Architect: Palmer Course Design Company
Interior Designer: Wilson & Associates, Cole Martinez Curtis and Associates
Contractor: Hensel Phelps Construction; ROEL Construction Co., Inc.
Photography: Robb Gordon; Mary E. Nichols; Peter Vitale; Four Seasons Hotels & Resorts

Hilton Hawaiian Village Beach Resort & Spa 160
Waikiki Beach, Honolulu, Oahu, Hawaii, USA
Client/Owner: Hilton Hotels Corporation
Architect: WATG
Landscape Architect: Woolsey, Miyabara & Associates, Inc.
Interior Designer: WATG; HBA/Hirsch Bedner Associates; Hilton Corp. Design Studio
Master Planner: WATG
Contractor: Albert C. Kobayashi, Inc.
Photography: Courtesy Hilton Hawaiian Village

Hilton Mauritius Resort & Spa 212
Wolmar, Flic en Flac, Mauritius, Africa
Client/Owner: Morning Light Co. Ltd.
Architect: WATG
Associate Architect: Francis Wong
Landscape Architect: Clarke Tongg McElvey
Interior Designer: Hirsch Bedner Associates
Contractor: Murray & Roberts Gamma Civic Joint Venture
Photography: Ogasawara Atomu; Christian Bossu-Picat; Eric Frigière; Bamba Sourang; Paul Wagner; Courtesy Hilton Mauritius Resort & Spa

Hilton Sanya Resort & Spa 32
Yalong Bay National Resort District, Sanya, Hainan, China
Client/Owner: China Jin Mao Group Co., Ltd.
Architect: WATG
Associate Architect: Shanghai Institute of Architectural Design and Research Co., Ltd.
Landscape Architect: Belt Collins International
Interior Designer: Chhada Siembieda Leung Ltd.
Contractor: Jin Mao Construction Ltd.
Photography: Courtesy Hilton Sanya Resort & Spa

Hong Kong Disneyland® Hotel 36
Lantau Island, Hong Kong, China
Client/Owner: Walt Disney Imagineering and Hong Kong SAR Government
Architect: WATG
Associate Architect: Ronald Lu Partners Hong Kong, Ltd.
Landscape Architect: Belt Collins, Hong Kong
Interior Designer: LRF, Hong Kong
Contractor: Shimizu Corporation/China State, (Joint Venture)
Photography: © Disney Enterprises, Inc.

Hyatt Regency Coolum 38
Coolum Beach, Queensland, Australia
Client/Owner: Kumugai Gumi Pty. Ltd.
Architect: WATG
Associate Architect: Bligh Robinson
Landscape Architect: Tongg Clarke & McCelvey
Golf Course Architect: Robert Trent Jones II
Interior Designer: HBA/Hirsch Bedner Associates
Contractor: Concrete Constructions Pty. Ltd.
Photography: Courtesy Hyatt Regency Coolum

Hyatt Regency Hua Hin 42
Hua Hin, Thailand
Client/Owner: Chai Talay Hotel Co Ltd
Architect: WATG
Associate Architect: Siam Syntech (SSC)
Landscape Architect: Peter Imrik, Site Concepts International
Interior Design: Carl Ettensperger; WATG
Photography: Courtesy Hyatt Regency Hua Hin

Hyatt Regency Huntington Beach Resort & Spa 268
Huntington Beach, California, USA
Client/Owner: Waterfront Development Inc.; The Robert Mayer Corporation
Architect: WATG

Interior Designer: KMA Designs, Inc.; WATG
Contractor: PCL Construction Services
Photography: Thomas Hinckley; Don Riddle; Paul Thompson; Paul Turang Photography

Hyatt Regency Jeju 44
Jeju Island, South Korea
Client/Owner: Namju Development Company
Architect: WATG
Associate Architect: Seoung Bae Shin
Landscape Architect: Tongg Clarke & Mechler; Seoin Design
Interior Designer: Chhada Siembieda & Associates, Ltd.
Contractor: ICC Construction Co., Ltd.
Photography: Courtesy Hyatt Regency Jeju

Hyatt Regency La Manga 138
Cartagena, Murcia, Spain
Client/Owner: Bovis Abroad Limited
Architect: WATG
Associate Architect: Jaime J. Bourne & Associates
Golf Course Architect: Arnold Palmer Design Company; David Thomas
Interior Designer: Gregory Aeberhard Design International, Updated in 2007 by Jaime Beriestain
Contractor: Bovis International Limited
Photography: Courtesy La Manga Club

Hyatt Regency Maui Resort & Spa 164
Kaanapali Beach, Lahaina, Maui, Hawaii, USA
Client/Owner: Maui Development Company/Host Marriott Corporation
Architect: WATG
Associate Architect: Lawton & Umemura, AIA
Landscape Architect: Tongg Clarke & McCelvey
Interior Designer: HBA/Hirsch Bedner Associates; Harry Stoff Interiors
Contractor: Hawaiian Dredging Company
Photography: Courtesy Hyatt Regency Maui Resort & Spa

Hyatt Regency Waikiki Resort & Spa 166
Waikiki, Oahu, Hawaii, USA
Client/Owner: Hemmeter Development Corporation
Architect: WATG
Associate Architect: Lawton & Taylor
Landscape Architect: Belt Collins
Interior Designer: WATG; Mary McCague Associates; Richard Crowell Associates
Contractor: Swinerton & Alberg Co.
Photography: Kyle Rothenborg, Rothenborg Pacific

InterContinental Jakarta MidPlaza 46
Jakarta, Indonesia
Client/Owner: InterContinental Jakarta MidPlaza
Architect: WATG
Landscape Architect: Belt Collins Associates
Interior Designer: James Northcutt / Wilson Associates
Contractor: PP Taisei
Photography: Courtesy InterContinental Jakarta MidPlaza

JW Marriott Hotel Beijing 48
Beijing, China
Client/Owner: Beijing Guo Hua Real Estate Ltd.
Design Architect: WATG
Local Architect: Huadong Architecture Design Institute Co. Ltd.
Landscape Architect: EDAW
Interior Designer: HBA Singapore
Contractor: Xinxing Construction Group
Photography: Courtesy Geoff Lung Photography

Pan Pacific Singapore   62
Singapore
Client/Owner: Pan Pacific Singapore
Original Architect: John Portman
Renovation Architect: WATG
Landscape Architect: Island and Landscape Pte Ltd.
Interior Designer: WATG; Dale Keller and Associates
Contractor: Hyundai Construction
Photography: Peter Mealin

Poets Cove Resort & Spa   276
South Pender Island, British Columbia, Canada
Client/Owner: Poets Cove Resort & Spa
Architect: Rositch Hemphill & Associates Architects
Landscape Architect: Arcon Rock and Waterscapes
Interior Designer: WATG
Photography: Courtesy Poets Cove Resort & Spa

Portofino Bay Hotel at Universal Orlando®, A Loews Hotel   278
Orlando, Florida, USA
Client/Owner: Universal Studios/ Rank Group Joint Venture/ Loews Hotels
Architect: WATG
Associate Architect: Morris Architects
Landscape Architect: Burton Associates
Interior Designer: Wilson & Associates
Photography: Courtesy Loews Hotels and Universal Orlando

Promised Land Resort & Lagoon   66
Shoufeng Township, Hualien, Taiwan
Client/Owner: PromisedLand Co., Ltd.
Architect: WATG
Associate Architect: C.H. Ho, International; Diligent Technical Associates; Universe International; Chien-Chung Chao Architect
Landscape Architect: TC&M
Interior Designer: Hendrikson Design
Contractor: RSEA
Photography: South Fish; Yu Liang Tasi; Chuan Wang; Courtesy PromisedLand Co., Ltd.

Renaissance Hollywood Hotel & Spa   280
Hollywood, California, USA
Client/Owner: TrizecHahn Development
Architect: WATG
Landscape Architect: SWA
Interior Designer: Cole Martinez Curtis
Contractor: Matt Construction
Photography: Courtesy Renaissance Hotels and Resorts International

Renaissance Tianjin TEDA Hotel & Convention Centre   68
Tianjin, China
Client/Owner: Grand Architects, Inc.; Tianjin Binhai TEDA Hotel Development Co., Ltd.
Architect: WATG
Associate Architect: Grand Architects Inc.
Landscape Architect: Grand Architects Inc.
Interior Designer: Grand Architects Inc.
Contractor: Grand Architects Inc.
Photography: Courtesy Renaissance Tianjin TEDA Hotel & Convention Centre

Sandalwood Private Resort   70
Hongqiao, Shanghai, China
Client/Owner: Shanghai Deluxe Family Estate Development Co., Ltd.
Architect/Interior Architect: WATG
Associate Architect: Henei Provincial Architectural Design & Research Institute
Landscape Architect: Belt Collins
Interior Designer: Hirsch Bedner Associates; Wilson & Associates; Graham Fayhe
Photography: Courtesy Shanghai Deluxe Family Estate Development Co., Ltd.

Sasakwa Lodge   226
Serengeti, Tanzania, Africa
Client/Owner: VIP Safari Club
Architect: WATG
Associate Architect: MD Consultancy
Landscape Architect: The Really Useful Landscape Company
Interior Designer: Interiors Designs Company Ltd.
Master Planner: WATG
Contractor: Murray & Roberts
Photography: Courtesy Singita Grumeti Reserves

Shangri-La Hotel, Singapore, Garden Wing   74
Singapore
Client/Owner: Shangri-La Hotel, Singapore
Architect: WATG
Associate Architect: Archiplan Team
Landscape Architect: Belt Collins Hawaii
Golf Course Architect: Belt Collins Hawaii
Interior Designer: Western International Hotels
Contractor: Paul Y. Construction (S) Pte. Ltd.
Photography: Courtesy Shangri-La Hotel, Singapore

Shangri-La's Barr Al Jissah Resort & Spa   232
Muscat, Oman
Client/Owner: The Zubair Corporation; Barr Al Jissah Resort Co. SAOC
Architect: WATG
Associate Architect: WS Atkins International & Co.
Landscape Architect: Landscape Designs
Interior Designer: Wilson & Associates
Contractor: Carillion Alawi LLC
Photography: George Mitchell

Sheraton Maui Resort   172
Kaanapali Beach, Maui, Hawaii, USA
Client/Owner: Kyo-ya Co. Ltd.
Architect: WATG
Landscape Architect: Walters Kimura Motoda, Inc.
Golf Course Architect: Robert Trent Jones II
Interior Designer: Sheraton Corporation; Barry Design Associates
Contractor: Swinerton Walberg Westgate & Tait; Hawaiian Dredging Construction Co.
Photography: Courtesy Sheraton Maui Resort

Sheraton Soma Bay   236
Red Sea, Egypt
Client/Owner: Soma Bay Hotel Company
Architect: WATG
Associate Architect: Arcadia
Landscape Architect: Canin Associates
Interior Designer: Thompson and Leggett
Contractor: Kajima Corporation
Photography: Soma Bay Hotel Company; Anthony Parkinson

CONTRIBUTORS

The people listed here have all worked in WATG's offices
and assisted in bringing to life the projects presented within these pages.

Peer Abben	Piotr Anisko	Amy Becker	Deborah Bowers	Shon Burton
Renee Abdessalam	Charles Apel	Luis Beckford	Nathalie Boyero	Bonifacio Butardo
Dean Abernathy	Vikram Apte	Frances G. Beckham	Nina Boyett	Dale Butler
Raymond Abeyta	Homeyra Arbabi	Michaela Bedari	Cynthia Boyle	C.E. Bye
Richelle Abiang	Storm Archer Iii	Matthew Beehler	Robert Boyle	Harold Byrde
Anna C. Abreu	Leandro Ardigo	Fikerte Befekadu	Scott Boyle	Brigid Byrne
Doug Ackerman	Kathleen Armstrong	Jennifer Belcher	Krista Boyte	Dedicacion Cabreros
John Ackerman	Indira Arnautovic	Christopher Belknap	Chris Bradley	Naidah Cabrido
Alberto Acuna	Gretchen Arnemann	David Bell	Gordon Bradley	Carolyn Calame
Catherine Adachi	Alma Arnold	Paul Belle	Ben Brady	Michael Calame
Joni S. Adahl	Pedro Arteche	Eusebio Bello	Kristan Braswell	Dean K. Caldarelli
Jeffrey Adair	Bernardo Artola	Kristina Benkovsky	Victoria Brenchley	Larry Calderon
Donald Adams	Rashid Ashraf	Marcia Benson	Mary-Jo Brennan	Silvio M. Calegari
Jennifer Adams	Jennifer Asselstine	George Berean	Paul Brestyansky	Bertine Callow
Siba Adom	Chad Asuncion	Zhanna Berenfeld	Steven Bretherton	Lucas Camacho
Ernesto Agaloos, Jr.	Charlotte Atkinson	David Berggren	Steven D. Brewer	Phillip Camp
Ellen Agcaoili	Mohammed E. Attia	Maureen Bergin	Allison Brill	Benjamin Candari
Jose Luis Ahumada	Bunny Au	Lining Berman	Lindsay Broad	Thomas Cannon
Peter Aiello	Charissa Au	Julie Berry	Cary Brockman	Christine Cano
Lois Ajifu	William Au	Alex I. Betancourt	Penelope Brocksen	Christy Canter
Rhiain Akin	Leticia Avalos	Ruben Betancourt	Judi Bronnert	Neil Capangpangan
Lee K. Ako	Natasha Ayala-DelRio	Josette Bevirt	Alex Brostek	Roberto Caragay
Melvin Ako	Tom Ayers	Sylvia Beyke	Dorothy Brown	Jennifer Caravalho
Peter Akran	Joey Ayson	Inderpal Bhogal	Gail E. Brown	Sarah Cardoza
Stephen Albert	Brooke Azumi	Patricia Biechler	Perry Brown	Beth Carlson
Amina Al Balushi	Lindon Bachelder	John Bigay	Rebecca Brown	Bradley Carlson
Bryan Algeo	Amanda Bageant	Neal D. Bilyeu	Samuel Brown	Kelly Carlson
Wais Karim Ali	Loretta Bageant	Andrea Binikos	Sandi Brown	Claire Carr
Mark Alleman	Yasamin Bahadorzadeh	Randy Bishop	Scott Brown	Nicholas Carrier
Jenna Allen	Fely Baisac	Tom Black	Victoria Brown	Lisa-Maree Carrigan
Mike Allen	Michael Bakemore	Catherine Blackburn	William Brown	Tamara Carroll
Frank Allison	Alysa Baker	Patrick J. Blackburn	Jerry Browning	Samuel Carson
Gerald 'Jerry' Allison	Jim Balding	Lisa Blair	Patricia Browning	Elise Carter
Lynn Allison	Robert Baldino	Yacira Blanco	Michael Brownlie	Roger Carter
Lama Alkhalifa	Pam Baldwin	Carla Bloom	Kelly Bruce	Lisa Case
Hala Alramadhi	Todd Balicki	Bruce Blouse	Susan Bruce	Oscar Castelo
David Alsop	Trixie Ballesteros	Andrew Bober	Cara Brunk	Paz Castelo
Cynthia Alvarez	Ronald Banco	Harold Bock	Joseph Bruno	Cesar Castillo
Lori Ann Amaki	Scott Barbour	Nicole Boelter	Keith Bryant	Judith C. Castillo
Murad Amlani	Danielle Barclay	Stella Bok	Julie Buckley	Giovanni Castor
Sharrise Amlani	Jill Barclay	Boanerges Bolanos	Samuel Budiono	Imelda Catlin
Melonie Anaston	Dan Barlev	Ewa Bolesta	Emmanuel Buenaventura	Richard Cerezo
Takahashi Ande	Lell Barnes	Deberoh Booher	Maria Bugarin	Curtis Chan
Patrick Andersen	Robert Barragan	Thanu Boonyawatana	Beth Buhrmester	Rajesh 'Raj' Chandnani
Mary Anderson	Sandra Barzilay	Adam L. Borchardt	Christopher Bunao	Candis Chang
Meghna Andley	Gilbert Basbas	Richard Bosch	Jim Burba	Henry Chang
Lorrin Andrade	Roy Bass	Stephen Bossart	Ian Burgess	Lindsay A. Chang
Concepcion Andres	Richard Batangan	Christopher Boswell	Ivana Burianova	Nancy Chang
Evelyn Ang	Rodney Batara	Burt Boucock	Katherine R. Burleson	Spencer Chang
Cecilia Angulo	Michael Batchelor	Lysanne Bourgouin	Kevin Burt	Terry Chang

Sarah Chapman
Sidney 'Sid' Char
Robin Chard
Michael R. Charters
Chi-Lou Cheang
Boisie Checa
Chau-Hsin Chen
Guan Chen
Janie Chen
Jenny Chen
Sam Chen
Sung-Cheng Chen
Yuan Zheng Chen
Jenny Chen-Eng
Feona Cheng
Rita Chen-Howard
Rachel Chesterfield
Douglas Cheung
Norman Cheung
Godofredo 'Doy' Chico
Gregory A. Childress
Jack Ching
Sharon Ching
Ion Chiose
Nancy Chitwood
Tat 'Alex' Cho
Owen Chock
Reuben Chock
Sunny Choi
Min Swee Choong
Canossa Choy
Mel Choy
David Christensen
Scott Christensen
Harris Christiaansen
Brandishea Christian
Nghe Chu
Catherine Chun
Jennifer Chun
Kathleen Chun
Kevin Chun
Michael Chun
Carol Chun-Craddock
Hanne Church
Bonnie Churchwell
Terrance Cisco
Jackie Clark
Jennifer G. Clark
Rachel Clark
Quinton Clark
Nina Claro-Cuyong
Jill Claus
Peter Clement
Christine Cline
Wayne Close
Christie Cobbett
Doug Cochran
Keith Cockett
Adam Coghill
Gregory Coghill
G. Cole
David Coloma
Jack Commander
Deanna Cone
Marie Connell
Sean Connelly
Walter Connors
Fred Cook
Howard Cook
P. Cook

Emma Cookson
Julian Coombs
Meg Corbett
Gregg Cornforth
Carolina Correa
Alan Corrigan
Jonathan Cort
Charles Corwin
Elizabeth Corwin
Arnel Costa
Mazeppa Costa
Page Costa
Robert Costa
Cheryl Costello
Robert Cox
Jennie Crabb
Cheryl Creber
Virginia Criley
Patrick Critton
Keith Crockett
Robert Crone
John Cropper
Mildred Crowson
William M. Crozier
Jose Cuadros
Monica Cuervo
Howard Culbreth II
Fiona Cumming
Lawrence Cunha
David Curry
Sandra Czerniak-Bye
Lizabeth Czerniel
Michael Czoik
Michelle D'Amico
Rachan Danapong
Zohreh Daneshvar
Vanessa N. Daniel
David Daniels
Melanie Daniels
Blaine D'Armond
Soumya Das Gupta
Cary Dasenbrock
Afroditi Daskalopoulou
Steven Datmagurun
Leon David
Tom David
Susanne Davidson
Isabelle Davis
Scott Davis
Stacie Davis
Stephane Davis
Victoria Davis
Virgil Davis-Planas
Patrick Dawson
Robert Day
Andrea De Camp
Alison De Castella
Thomas De Costa
Kathie De Leon
Maurice De Leon
Mike De Podesta
Polly DeBlank
Thomas Deem
Antonia DeFonte
Paul Degenkolb
Supranee Degraw
Cida Deguchi
Jeanette Deighan
Rodrigo Del Carpio
Mario Delamerced
Luis Delance

Iluminada Delos Santos
Luciano G. DeLuca
Adam Demetriou
Jill Den Hartog
Dan Deselm
Jessica Dessing
Cesare F. Di Battista
Paolo Diaz
Devon J. Dickerson
Christy Diecker
J. Ascenzo Digiacomo
Kelly Dignan
David Dike
Rodrigo Dimla
Bala S. Dirisala
John Dixon
Flora Djoenaedi
Travis Do
Tri Dinh Do
Dimitri Dobrescu
Nathan L. Dobson
Nicole M. Dobson
Susie Dobson
Janice Doering
Alexis Dolan
Robert Dollar
Shawn Dolley
Stephanie Domingo
Rosie Dominic
Michael Donahue
Laura L. Dondero
Margaret Donohoe
Elizabeth Doran
Amanda Douglas
Lynn Dow
David Drake
Shaun Drummond
Stacey Drummond
Francois Du Toit
Sarah C. Ducote
Niki Duffy
Dawn Dunbar
Charles Dundas-Shaw
Robert Dunford
Matthew Dungan
Kathryn Dunker
Gerald Dunn
Patrick Durkin
Anna Dutton
Peter Dykstra
Jesus Eballar
Marla B. Echeverria
John Edwards
Sean Edwards
Lydia Jane Egan
Karen Eichman
Divina Elefante
Fedaa I. El-Dosougi
Michael Eliades
John Elliott
Kelsey Elliott
Tehri Elliott
Rebecca Ellis
Marina Ellison-Nyerges
Courtney Embrey
Suzette Emerson
Maggie Emery
Holly Enete
Kurtis Eng
Bruce E. Engmann

Scott Ericson
Laura Escarcega
Ignacio Escribano
Sherry Eshenbaugh
Erin Espeland
Raul Espiritu
Ilustre Estrella
Carl Ettensperger
Rosauro Eva, Jr.
Manuel Evalle
Anna Marie Evans
Christopher Evans
Julie Evans
Scott Ezer
Bruce Fairweather
Donald Fairweather
JaneMarie Fajardo
Farnaz Faraji
Scott Fares
Thomas Fee
Leslie Feeney
Marjory Feher
David Fellows
Rebecca Felman
Wenfei Feng
Gerald Ferguson
Augusto Fernandez
Laura Fernandez
Ruby Fernandez
Doug Fesler
Jenni Field
Bryan Figueira
Krista Findlay
Kristen Finley
Elizabeth Fink
Steve Fischer
Al Fisher
Jean Fisher
Joni Fisher
Ried Fisher
Lyn Fitzhugh
Lee Ann Fleming
Bryan Flores
Thomas Fo
Randall Fong
Renee Fontaine-saint-clair
Lynne Ford
Monica Forsyth
Leilani Fortuno
Lorraine Foster
Geoffrey Fox
Robert Fox
Emmanoel Francisco
Mary Ann Frank
Stanley J. Frank III
John Franz
James Freeman
Vicente Frias
Susan Frieson
Dean Fukawa
Arnold Fukunaga
Jay Fulton
Louis Fulton
Jason Fung
Vince Fusco
Al Gabay
Gabrielle M. Gabbert
James P. Gabbriellini
Elizabeth Gaidos
Jeffrey Gaither

Lyndon C. Galut
MariaRica D. Galut
Barbara Ganson
Ge Gao
Jeff Feng Gao
Jose A. Garavito
Julie Garcia
Karen Garcia
Nora Garcia
Jennifer Gardner
Rosemarie Garganta
Conrad Garner
Neil Garratt
Howard Garris
Michael Ray Garris
Jay B. Gaspar
Roger Gaspar
Mary Gaudet
Erin Gebo
Ursula Gehrmann
Lisa Gellen-League
Patricia Geminell
Michael Gentile
Wendy George
Natalie Geue
Celia Geyer
Sara Geyer
Raad Ghantous
Giancarlo Giacchi
Robert Gibson
Emma Gibson-Smith
Gary Gidcumb
Ramona Giesbrecht
Kirsty Gill
Sherry Gill
Juan C. Gimeno
Sandra Giorgetti
Patrick Girvin
Toowlys L. Gnabo
Christopher Go
Lisa Gobeo
Robin Goddard
John Goldwyn
Richard Gomez
Cathy Gonzales
Maria Gonzales
Ausberto Gonzalez
Gloria Gonzalez
Leopoldo Gonzalez
Barbara Goo
Debbie Goo
Donald Goo
Wayne Goo
Robert J. Good
Tina Goodwin
Alexander Gordon
Matthew Gorodinsky
Sandey Gorodinsky
Lee Gott
John Gould III
James Grady
Jenni Grafham
Rena Graham
Renate Granitzer
Benjamin Grant
John Grant
Andrea Grassi
Frank Gratton
Deeann Gray
Ashley Green
Deborah Green

Georgette Green
Jennifer Greenwald
Andreas Grieg
Daniel Griffin
Pamela Gring
Gail Gronau-Brown
Scott T. Gross
Gerald Grossman
Jim 'Kimo' Guequierre
André Guerrero
William Gulstrom
Richard Gumayagay
Dori Gusman
Josue Gutierrez
An Ha
Thoai Ha
Neil Haarhoff
Boris C. Haase
Mary Haase
Thomas Haeg
Scott Haeseker
Marian Haggerty
Tanya Hagiwara
Samina Haider
N. Robert Hale
Craig Hall
Sara Hall
Shashikanth Hallibyl
Liz Hallin
Brendan Halloran
Simeon Halstead
Lynn E. Hamada
Jennifer Hammer
Nicole Hammond
Yvette Hampton
Elaine Han
James Handsel
George Handy
Cheri Hanna
Shaun Hannah
Ainslee Hansen
Edith Hara
John Harada
Diane Hardie
Nicole Harouche
Alethea Harris
Ian Harris
Norman Harris
Fritz Harris-Glade
Engel Harrop
Sean C. Harry
Horace Hartman
James Harty
Mildred Harvey
Nazie Hashemi
Lori Hass
Mark Hastert
Sandra Hatchett
David Hayes
Edward Haysom
Jennifer E. Hawkins
Gregory Hee
Selina Heer
John Heineman
Larry Helber
David Henderson
Francine Henderson
Maureen Hendricks
Pamela Hendrickson
Alice Henselman
Kathleen Herbage

Felicia Herrick
Lucy Heslop
Jeremy Heyes
Tracey Hickler
Betty Hickok
Alisa Hicks
John Hicks
Elizabeth Higa
Mark Higa
Jack Highwart
Laura Hill
Lois Hiram
Ray Hirohama
Wendy Hisashima
Sheila Hixenbaugh
Inga Hjartardottir
Lawrence Ho
Mary Hoang
Wendy T. Hoffman
Kim Hoite
Scott P. Holcomb
Ronald Holecek
Michelle Holiday
Christina Holland
Lynne Holley
Katherine Hollingsworth
Melissa Hollingsworth
Lars Holm
Daniel Hong
Frederick Hong
Sunyoung 'Sunny' Hong
Yu Hong
Ila Hoopai
Cynthia Hope
Carol Hopkins
Rory Hopkins
Stacy Hoppes
James Horman
Charles Horne
Mike Hounslow
Rosy Howard
Frances L. Howell
Katie Hoyt
Jonathan Z. Hradecky
Anne Hritzay
I-Ming Hsiue
Chi-Yen Huang
Haibo Huang
Raymond Huang
Dawn Hubbard
Donna Hubbard
Kam Huckins
M. Hueftle
ChunWah Hui
YuFung B. Hui
Jill Huizing
Bent Huld
Bryant Humann
Allen Hung
Perry Hung
Mavis Hunnisett
Heber Hurd
Jesus Hurtado
Iqbal Hussain
Brian Husting
Concepcion Ibanez
Joanne Ibanez
Jennifer Impellizeri
Susan Ings

Arkanit Intarajit
Puangthong Intarajit
Robert Iopa
Sondra Isbell
Christopher Isbister
Leigh Ishida
Ra'ana Islam
Rafique Islam
Meagan Jacobi
Ariel Jacobs
Cynthia Jacobs
Joseph Jacobs
Ruben Jaictin
Mukesh K. Jain
Colin James
Tammy James
Cristina Janigan
Monika Jaroszonek
Bradford Jencks
Kenneth Jenkins
Sih-Young 'Sean' Jeon
Laura E. Jew
Dae Soo Ji
Shan Jin
Derry-Lynn John
Francis Johnson
James Johnson
Jennifer Johnson
Jon Johnson
Lon Johnson
Lynne Johnson
Michael Johnson
Nilda Johnson
Rachel E. Johnson
Shirley Johnson
Christopher Jones
Paul Jones
Brian Jowett
Debra Joyce
Natalia Juliano
Jennifer Kaatz
Neil Kahn
Carole Kajiwara
Kenneth Kajiwara
Christine Kakour
Christian Kaleiwahea
Arash A. Kamangar
Shirley Kanahele
Laura Kanazawa
Daniel Kanekuni
Anne Kanemoto
Denise Kaneshiro
Jason Kaneshiro
Kay Kaneshiro
Arvind Kannan
William Kanotz
Gran C. Kao
Stephanie Kapanui
Alexa Kapioltas
Judith Kaplan
Ioannis Kappos
Barry Karim
Milan Karlovac
Kim Karmozyn
Mark Kasarjian
Ken Kashimoto
Kurt Katada
Mina Kato
Susan Cain Katz
Misako Kawakami
Dean Kawamura

Nancy Au Kawanoue
Stanley Kawasaki
Vrej Kayekjian
Steven Kearns
Reyna Keaunui
Rosemary Keefe
Linda M. Kelley
Lee Kellum
Nicky Kelly
Kathleen Kelm
Nils Kenaston
Brett Kennerley
Kelley Kesinger
Gregory Kessler
Sunchai Keuysuvan
Francik Khalili
Abdullah Khan
Fazal Khan
Rumman Khan
Dalinda Khuon
Michael R. Kidde
Neal Kido
Ahkyeong Kim
Ashley Kim
Brandon Kim
David Kim
Dennis Kim
Gee Kim
JongWoo Kim
NaJung Kim
Naomi Kim
Sophia Kim
Sung-Min Kim
YongGi Kim
Glenn Kimura
Lucille Kimura
Alene King
Jacqueline King
Pamela Kisow
Anton Kisselgoff
Akiko Kitahara
Robert Kleinkopf
Jeanie Kleuter
Robert Kleven
Chris Knight
Clive Knight
HwangJin Ko
Hideo Kobayashi
Laureen Kodama
Jan J. Kofranek
Marcella Kofranek
Justin Koizumi
Katie Kollmansberger
Ellery Komenaka
Janek R. Konarski
Lesley-Anne 'Puna' Kondo
Olivier Koning
Richard Koob
Elaine Kopinga
Karl Korth
Kemal Koseoglu
Koizumi Kotaro
George Koteles
Alexandra Kotsos
Mark Kowalski
Charlene Kowblick
Jin Koyama
Mikako Koyama
Dorothy Krause
Andrea Krejcik

Connie Kruayai
Jon Krueger
Patrick Kruger
Stanley Kruse
Colleen Kunishige
Caroline Kuo
Leslie Kurasaki
Suzan Kushiyama
Ronald Kwan
Henry Kwok
Kevin La
Zernan Labay
Gary Lacno
Santos Martin Lacuesta
Joan Lafountaine
Kapil Lahoti
Devin Lai
Albert Lam
Amy Lam
Andrew Lam
Clemson Lam
May Lam
Manuel Lamarche
Matthew Lamb
Sharon Lang
Erin Langan
James Langan
Suzanne Lange
Kandra Lapinta
Robert Larsen
Ingrid Larsson
Andy W. Lau
Charles Lau
Elena Lau
Johnny Lau
Julie Lau
Karen Lye Leng Lau
Marianne Lau
J. Patrick Lawrence
Andrew Lawson
C. Lawson
Leonilo Laxa
Khoi Le
Peter Le
Vu Le
Leslie Le Bon
Philippa Le Roux
Anna Lee
Annie M. Lee
Chang Lee
Darren Lee
Donald Lee
Edna Lee
Fung Ping 'Marlene' Lee
Gary Lee
Hideko Tanaka Lee
Joann Lee
JungKum Lee
Lisa Lee
Tiffany Lee
Yo Han Lee
Geoffrey Leggett
Seth A. Leimgruber
Mary Ellen Lenander
Cindy Lenart
Pedrito Leong
John Leopardi
Jack Leung-How
Karen Levesque

Reiko Lewis
Stacy Lezaja
Janice Yk Li
Margaret Li
Xiaomin Li
Bob Liao
Feliciano Libao
Daniel M. Lieberman
Bob Liebsack
Jennifer Lien
Lori Liermann
Yoke-Peng Liew
Sarah Lim
Thomas Lim
Robertino Limandibhratha
Silpa Limbachia
RenYng Lin
Hung-Tsung Lin
John David Lindsay
Tom Litaker
Jen-Jiunn Liu
Ke Liu
Shannon Liu
Wei-Chi Liu
Catherine Liuzzi
Marc Lizama
Romela Lloren-Talusan
Christopher Lloyd
James Loft
Betty Loh
Wai-Kai Lok
Dora Lokietek
Claudio Lopes
Enrique Lopez
Harold Lopez
Daniel Loriot
Aneska Lotter
Carolyn Loughrey
Sharon Louthen
Lai Kuen Low
Edith R. Lucas
Noland Lucas
Jose Luciano
John Ludlow
Herb Luke
Sherilyn Lum
Sherry Lun
Kyle Lung
Jennifer Lutz
Christine Luu-Rowe
Paul Lyons
Paul Stuart Lyons
Chi-Hung Ma
Nilo Mabunay
Deborah Mace
Grace Machado
Marcia Mack
Ross Mackenzie
Maureen MacKinnon
Jeffrey MacNeill
Maureen Madigan
Celeste Madrigal
R. Maeda
Keith Maekawa
Lynden Maekawa
Robby Mago
Lisa M. Malenfant
Monica Malhotra
Edgardo Mallari
Massimo Mallia

Kin-Ming Man
Matius Mandolang
Philip Mangonon
Rohit Mankar
Heather Mann
Thomas Manok
Mohamed Mansour
Sagar Mansukh
Danna Mao
Meagan Marchant
Rocky Marquez
Cynthia Marr
Douglas W. Marsh
Bude Martin
Candice Martin
Shannon Martin
Christin Martinelli
Catherine Martinez
Eduardo Martinez
Harvey Maruya
F. Marvin
Sharrise Masaki-Amlani
Michelle Masuda
Eric Matsumoto
John Matsumoto
Toshiko Matsushita
Robert Mattox
R. Mau
Ross Maxwell
Stephanie May
Fayez Mazid
Richard McAllister
Roberta McCabe
Greg McCants
Stefanie McCarron
Kathleen McClafferty-Logue
Jesse McClurg
Michal McComas
J. Marie McCormick
Megan L. McCrary
Martha McCullough
Purnima McCutcheon
Victoria McDonald
Andrew McGarry
Muriel McGrath
Peter McGurk
Jacqui McIver
Michael McKay
Diane McLeod
Pamela McMullen
Rueko McNally
Bradford McNamee
Nicole McPhee
John McQuown
Karen Mead
Alexander Meave
Silvia Medvidova
Vicki Meece
Louise Mellish
Sonja Melton
Tony Menezes
Miguelito Mercado
Shirley Mercado
Israel Mercedes
Melissa Merrell
Nina Merrell
Caralyn Merrill
Adam Metel
Elaine Metler

B. Meyers
Margaret Ann Michels
Lauren Michioka
Svetlana Micic
Diane Midgely
John Miesen
Fred Mikawa
Andrea Miles
Sonya Miles
Mitchell Millar
Vicki Millard
Cindy Miller
Karen Miller
Kim Mills
Michael Milo, Jr.
Christine Minassian
Peggy Minger-McCants
Aaron Minson
Mohamed Mirza
Radha Mistry
Lauren Mitchell
Linda Mitchell
Ronald Mitchell
Ron Mitori
Tom Mitrano
Kazuhiko Miwa
Gary Miyakawa
Carrie Miyasato
Janice Miyoshi-Vitarelli
Sharon Mizuno
Jonathan Mizzi
Dale Moen
Susan Moises
D. Molegraaf
Katherine Monge
Hoover Monleon
John Montierth
Frank Montillo
Mary Montoya
David Moore
James Moore
William Moore
Brenda Moors
Milford Moralde
Ernesto Morales
Susan Morgan
Katherine Moriarty
Salli Morita
Steven Morita
Caroline Mormino
Adam Morris
Doug Morris
Mitchell Morris
Jafar Mosleh
Bruce Mosteller
Alica Mryglod
Joyce Mullin
Maeriel Mumpar
Marie Mundheim
Alan Murakami
Grant Murakami
Arun Muralidhar
Craig Murayama
Virginia Murison
Gary Murphy
Hal Murphy
Julia Murphy
James Murray
Samantha Murray

Alexander Muttscheller
Richard Myers
Clint Nagata
Jann Nagato
Ronald Nakagawa
Mark Nakahira
Stephen Nakamitsu
Jeffrey Nakamura
Liane Nakamura
Lonnie Nakasone
William Nakayama
John Naleyanko
Dayna Nam
Nadi Nammar
Robert Napack
Jeffrey Naprawa
Michael Narciso
Rose Ann Nash
Nevine Nasser
Sally Nava
Ashley N. Nelson
Paul Nelson
Stephen Nemeth
Shantel Neo Yen Peng
Carly Nesbitt
Deepak Neupane
Jennifer Neupane
Laura Newman
Erich Newson
Kai Lin Ng
Lester Ng
Oon Tian Ng
Ivy Ngeow
Long D. Nguyen
Mary Nguyen
Nick Nguyen
Son Nguyen
Huy Nhan
Amauri Nicasio
Patricia Nicholas
Charles Nield
Paul Niiyama
Darrell Nilles
Lindsay Nishii
Nancy Nishikawa
Robin Nishimura
Homero Nishiwaki
Carolyn Noland
Timothy Nomer
Bill Nord
Darryl Nordstrom
Todd Nordstrom
Christine A. Norris
Pamela Norton
April Nottage
Andrew Nyerges
Homer Oatman
Laura Oatman
Leonora Obispo
Jean Olvey
Taidg O'Malley
Dawn Onaga
Shirley Ong Pui Hoon
Christine Optiz
Merrilee Orcutt

Michael Ortega
Katherine Orthman
Ronald Ortiz
Bryce Osborn
Ernest Oshiro
Marisa Oshiro
Tracy G. Oshiro
Diana Osman
Scott Osterhage
Scott Ostrowski
Lori Oumaye
Gilbert Oviedo
Linda Owens
Alison Pace
Marcel Padomas
John Page
Matthew Page
Emily Pagliaro
Andria Pak
Karla Palma
Perla Palombo
Sunit Panchal
Michael Paneri
Christina Pang
Rolando Panganiban
Christina Pang-Capello
Adrienne Paniagua
Nick Paniagua
Carrie Pannick-Reyes
Florencio 'Spyder' Paraon
James Paresi
James Park
John Park
Sooyoun Park
YoungKyu Park
Deborah Parks
N. Parnes
Elizabeth Paskalidis
Mark Paskill
Mita P. Patel
Payal Patel
Ramesh Patel
Sagar Patel
Shanna Patel
Stefan Pateman
Purnima Patil-McCutcheon
Geoff Patterson
Erik Duff Paulsen
Daniel Paun
Ilie Paun
James Pawlowicz
Sylvia Pawlowski
Robert Payan
Derry-Lynn Payn
Bernard Pebenito
Cathy Pechstedt
Noe Pegarido
Chun-Yen Peng
Joe Peng
Rachel Penn
Troy Pennington
Enrique Pepino
Anne Perez
Joelle Perez
M. Perry
Jana E. Pesek
Alexia Petridis
Danny Pham
Jon Pharis

Amanda Philips
Joan Michele Phillips
Richard Phillips
Wanda Phillips
Apinant Phuphatana
Gordon Pickering
Kandice Pierce
Andrea Piper
Abena Poku
Daniel Polkinhorn
Mark Pollard
Catherine Pollock
Amber Poltl
Udom Pongsawat
Susan Poole
Daniel Popovici
Mihai Popovici
Allan Porter
Jack Potamianos
Kirk Potter
Azita Pourmehr-Quon
Nick Poynton
Darmawan Prawirohardjo
Lee Preece
Vic Preuveneers
Stacy Prince
Brian Prock
Kiranjit Puaar
John Pugh
Candice Pulliam
Daniel Pun
Shirley Pyun
Angela Quiason
Manolo Quiason
Tricia Quiason
Teresa Quincey
Tina Quintana
Suzanne Rabey
Kay Radzik
Delbert Ragland
Hyon Rah
Anthony Ramirez
Mariano Ramirez
Carl Ramos
Humberto Ramos
Shakti Raol
Lori Rapport
Vikki Raschbacher
Rhonda Rasmussen
Guy Ratcliffe
Kathleen Rawnsley
Chad Raynes
Marcelino Raza
Bruce Reay
Scott Redfield
Emma Redor
Mandy Reed
William Reed
Richard Reep
Jill Reider
Shelley Reiner
Missy Jo Renard
Nancy Reno
Art Reola
Victoria Reventas
Alena M. Reyes
Heather Reynolds
Melanie Richards
Nathaneal Richards
Sarah Richardson

Carol Rieck
Paul Ries
Jennie Ringer
Daniel Riordan
Nancy I. Rios
Andre Riou
Nathaniel Rivera
Andrew M. Rivlin
Giselle M. Rizzardi
Scott Robart
Emily Roberts
Erin Roberts
Barry Robinson
Marcus Robinson
Keith Robishaw
Susan Robkin
Eduardo Robles
Victor Robles
Elizabeth Rocha
Larry Rocha
David Rodrigues
Kimberly Rodrigues
Gabriel Rodriguez
J. Lee Rofkind
Deborah Rogger
Nilufer Rohleder
Luis Roman
Elizabeth Rosas
Mayra Rosas
Michael Rosen
Laura Rosenberg
Deborah Rosenblum
Paul Rosero
Suling V. Roth
Katherine Rothrock
Allen Rothschild
Maurie Rouchard
Donal Rounds
Rosemary Rowan
Anna M. Roxo
Pauline Roy
Jennifer Rubio
Emma Ruddock
Hanna Rude
Pamela Rudin
Josianne Ruel
Prudencio Rumbaoa
Lotte Rundqvist
Patrick Russel
Tom Russell
Kirsty Rutherford
Lila Ruzicka
Helen Ryan
Jeff Sabini
Edie Sagarang
Dennis Sagucio
Erin Sagucio
Ray Sagun
Caryn Saito
Tatsuo Saito
Wendell Sakagawa
Michael Salerno
Gregorio Salinas, Jr.
Gary Saling
Pablo Salomon
William Salter
Richard Salvato
Steven Samuelson
Michael Samuleman
Daniel Sandomire

Pirasak Sanguanmitr
Patrick Sanjongco
Vicki Sansone-
    Kirchgassner
Nemencio Santos
Reynaldo Santos
Dennis Sapphire
Atilano Saradpon
Ting Saradpon
Eric Sargeant
Daniel Sauerbrey
Michelle Saunders
Adrian Savany
Marios Savopoulos
Helen Saw
Wade Scaramucci
Robert Schaeffer
Dorothy Schafer
Anna Schef
Thomas Schmidt
James Schmit
Helen Schofield
Kevin Scholl
Marlene Schwartz
Ashley Sciore
Jennifer Scott
Kathryn Scott
Peter Scott
Patti Seay
Lydia Seeley
Nathan Sellenriek
Peter Seo
Yosesh Seth
Lesellier Severine
Michael Seyle
Beth Shafer
Thomas Shaffer
Jayna Shah
Pankaj Shah
Preksha Shah
Leslie Shammas
Ali Shams
Raghavendra
    Shanbhag
Meenakshi Sharma
James Sharp
Donald Shaw
Ralph Shelbourne
Katie Sheldrick
Clive Shepherd
Brett Shepperson
Dennis Sheridan
Han Shi
Tracey Shiau
Emi Shiga
Vincent Shigekuni
Colin Shimokawa
Janine Shinoki
Moses Shirai
Dale Shishido
Douglas Shoemaker
Caron Shore
David Shu
Kirsten Siebenhaar
Justin Sigrist
Eduardo Silva
Jennifer Silva
Del Simon
Charles Sims
Crispolo Sindiong

Christopher Singer
Luis Sison
Joseph Sistler
B. Skadsheim
Paul Slater
Thomas Smail
Christopher Smirnoff
Bradley Smith
Curetis Smith
Darren Smith
Eric Smith
Kylene Smith
Lisa Smith
Lori A. Smith
Nicola Smith
Nicole Smith
Ryan Smith
Maica Smith-Belknap
Valentine Snell
Thomas Snodgrass
Mitzi Snyder
Sybrina Soga
Maria Solomon-Hirao
Krystal Solorzano
Emma Somers
Norman Soohoo
Elias Soto
Brian Spahr
Kate Spencer
Diana H. Stacey
Stephen Stafford
Starr Stallings
Luz Stam
Gavin Stanley-
    Grossman
Jeanne Starling
Jessica L. Steiner
Sarah S. Steiner
Robert Stempner
Jan Stenberg
Agneta E. Stephenson
Angelica Stern
Robert Stern
Sandy Stern
Rae Stevens
Cindy Stewart
Amy Stillman
Edie Stilwell
Chad Stith
Timothy Stoaks
Lucija Stojevic
Stella Stojic
Ivory Chris Stokes
Jason Stooks
Diana Stoyanova
Jennifer Strafford
Audrey Strapple
L. Strauss
Martin Stuart
Rhonda Stueber
Karl Stumpf
Lloyd Sueda
Karen Suenaga
Mary Suenaga
Shannon Suess
Jeanne Sullivan
LaleLisya Sullam
Kate Sultan
Sham Summan
Guthery Summer

Djuan Summerville
Ruoyun Sun
David Sung
Nopmanee
    Supsoontornkul
John Suska
Patrick Sutton
Robert Sutton
Douglas Swank
Arlyn Sweesy
Glenn Sweesy
Leanna M. Swenson
Torsten Symonds
Ellen Tabbons
Daren L. Tackis
Garrett Tagawa
Elissa Tajon
Bret Takahashi
Craig Takahata
Stanley Takaki
Gerald Takano
Dorene Takenaka
Joni Takenaka
Serenity Talbot
Shireen Talhouni
Joyce Tamanaha
Keith Tamura
Vince Tamura
Kuang-Wei Tan
Xiaosi Tan
Kelley Tanaka
Samuel Tang
Yu-Ping Tang
Sharmila Tankha
Vassil Tanouchev
Rolando Tapia
Dennis Tarampi
Jackie Tarrant
Susan Tasaki
Ann Tashiro
Chantelle Tate
Mark Tawara
Brett Taylor
Lyrica Taylor
Melissa Temples
Thomas Tengan
Evelyn Tenorio
Natalia Teo
Alan Teoh
Nestor Terrill
Cliff Terry
Jyoti Thanki
Clark Thiel
John Steven Thiersch
James Thomassen
Mark Thomassen
Andrew Thompson
Ann Thompson
Enwood Thompson
Marissa Thompson
Justyn Thornton
Nigel Thorsby
Jennnifer L. Timpe
Robert Tindall
Henry Ting
Katie Toboja
Traci Toguchi
Lisa Tokumaru
Sharie Tokumoto
Claire Tokunaga

G. Tokuno
Joann Toledo
Lynn Toma
Mike Toma
Rowenah Tomas
Brett Tomer
Simon Tomlinson
Cathy Tondelli
Gregory Tong
Vanessa Tonge
Hector L. Torres
Reynaldo Torres
Randy Totel
Anne Tovatt
Dao Tran
Levu N. Tran
Thuan Tran
Tuan Tran
Jesika Tran-Nguyen
Ian Trenowden
Thahn Tat Trinh
Lisa Troke
Christine Truxaw
Rebecca Trybus
Shirley Tsang
Pamela Tse
Cynthia Tsugawa
Justin Tucker
Sean Tully
Siri Tumpunyawat
Bonnie J. Tung
Ismet Turkalp
Emre Turkmen
Genevieve Turmel
Anglier Turner
Calvin Turner
Terry Tusher
Tammy Tuttle
Nile Tuzun
Chris Tyler
Alexander Uahihui
Daniel Ubovich
Yurica Ueda
Thomas Uemoto
Benjamin Ugale
Lex Ulibarri
Janina I. Umali
E. Umemoto
Robert Umemura
Jeanne Ung
Kristy Unger
Susan Uno
Laura Usherwood
Joyse Utick
Ronald Uyesugi
Gail Uyetake
Farrokh Vahid
Jan L. Vail
Sandra B. Vajcs
Holly Valentine-
    Steinhoff
James Valentine
Elham Valikhani
Jason Van Auker
Cheryl Ann Van Berkel
Margot Van Heerden
Richard Van Horn
Ronald Van Pelt
Tom Van Pelt
Anthony Van Strauhal

Jason Vanbruaene
Angela Van-De-Velde
Lisa Varela
John Vargas
Pat B. Varongsurat
Gabriel Vasquez
Joaquin Vasquez
Leonardo Velandia
Alba T. Velazquez
Leroy Velasquez
Rafael Velazquez
Maria I. Veleva
Valerie Velves
Brian Veneble
Sarah Venter
Marc Ventura
Jon Veregge
Carol Vesco
Rudolfo Victorio
Alexander Viernes
Micah Viernes
Ricardo Viernes
Roberto Viggayan
Greg Villegas
Maria Villegins
Aileen Vince-Cruz
Tracy Vincent
Eric Vinson
Vera L. Vizcarra
Ponn Paul Virulrak
Mindy Vo
Mark Vogt
Dawn Vojtush
Marivic T. Volack
Keir Vondruska
Cornelis Von
    Mollendorff
Deirdre Vouziers
Shannon Wadsworth
Jolie Wah
Jennifer Wakazuru
Charissa Walker
Kimberly Walker
Charles Wallace
Rondi Wallace
Christopher Walling
Graham Walsh
Hillary 'Lalo' Walsh
Thomas Walsh
Mark Walter
George Walters
Jonathan Wang
Lan Wang
Marcy Wang
Sheri Wang
Tracy Wang
Cheryl Ward
Jennifer Ward
Angela Wareham
Stephanie B. Warfield
Cindy Wasserman
Eugene Watanabe
Linda Watanabe
Vikki Waterbury
Douglas Waterman
Martin Waterman
Dionne Watkins
Leslie Watson
Donna Watson-
    Rossmoore

Alisa Weaver
Scott Weaver
Marion Weeber
ShouJung Wei
David Weisberg
John Weitz
Robert Wenkham
Adam Werfelmann
Amy Wert
Julia Wetherell
Stephanie Whiddon
George Whisenand
Loy Whisenand
Daniel White
Kimberly White
Sabine White
Mark Whitehouse
John Wiersma
Shanita Wiggins
Colin Wild
Garrett Wilkinson
Michelle Willey
Darlene Williams
Douglas G. Williams
Eugene Williams
Megan Williams
Michael Williams
Thomas Williams
Soh-Hyon Wilson
Suzanne Wilson
Wimberley Wilson
George 'Pete'
    Wimberly
Heather Wimberly
Matthew Winchester
Matthias Winkler
Jo Winter
Angelica A.
    Wirasandjaja
Airie Wise
Tom Witaker
Anna Witmer
Jessica Wolf
Howard Wolff
Willard Won
Christine Wong
Miranda Wong
Robert Wong
Stanley Wong
Flora Wong Chang
David Woo
Jennie Wood
Nadia J. Wood
Tom Wooge
Steven Worthington
Michelle Wright
Sharon Wright
Henry Thanh Wu
Jay Wu
Thelma Wurm
Charles Wyse
Kurt Xu
Serena Xu
Dani Yafuso
Jennifer Yagi
Dean Yama
Clarice Yamada
Jan Yamamoto
Ross Yamamoto
Roy Yamamoto

Corinne Yamasaki
Brett Yamashita
Maggie Yan
Rex Yang
Woo Seok Yang
Jia Yao
Chew Leng Yap
I-Chin Yi
Lican Ying
Catherine Yohn
Ross Yokoyama
Sheri Yonamine
Kevin Yoneda
Robert Yoneoka
Soo-Hyun Yoon
Brent Yoshida
Logan Yoshida
Mark Yoshizaki
Kellie Yost
Nancy Yost
Lisa Youk
Allison Young
Anastassia V. Young
Elizabeth Young
Kevin Young
Lawrence Young
Lori Young
Richard Young
Donna Yuen
Alexander Zabrodsky
Rashana Zaklit
Kasey Zantos
Dima A. Zatar
Richard L. Zatta
Martin Zauruskas
Sorin Zdrahal
Brigitte Zechner
Amor Zendejas
Dulka Zendejas
Sarah Zenti
Can Zheng
Chao 'Robert' Zheng
Zhaoyan Zheng
Donald Ziebell
Kelly Ziegler
Hongliang Zou

ACKNOWLEDGMENTS

by **Howard J. Wolff, Editor**

On behalf of WATG, thanks go to several key groups of people:

To WATG clients, who honor us by assigning their dreams to our drawing boards (and computer screens).

To WATG's team members, who work tirelessly to lift the spirits of hotel and resort guests whom they will never see.

To the dozens of fine photographers whose images bring the destinations on these pages to life.

To the talented professionals from the many design, engineering, and construction firms with whom we collaborate.

Several individuals deserve special thanks, as well:

Margaret Ann Michels worked diligently to manage the process of gathering materials and verifying their accuracy. Elisabeth Case and Katie Burleson contacted clients to ensure we had the latest and greatest images and information. They were assisted by Kristan Braswell, Ivana Burianova, Jennifer Chun, Robin Clewley, Steven Datmagurun, Leo Gonzalez, Dean Kawamura, Kara Morita, Abena Poku, and Cindy Wasserman. Jana Pesek provided valued expertise in art direction, photo editing, page layouts, and graphic design.

Jana Wolff wrote many of the project descriptions in this book and was a principal contributor to two previous collections of the firm's work, as well. Michael Rubin and Mary Scoviak, who wrote essays for this book, are both long-time friends of the firm, respected hospitality professionals, and exceptionally good at what they do.

Last and first thanks go to Alessina Brooks and Paul Latham at The Images Publishing Group, who not only thought WATG's earlier book was worthy of the title *Designing the World's Best Resorts* but also felt that it deserved a sequel.

ALGERIA | AMERICAN SAMOA | ANGUILLA | ANTIGUA | ARGENTINA | ARUBA | AUSTRALIA | AUSTRIA | AZERBAIJAN | BAHAMAS | BAHRAIN | BANGLADESH | BARBADOS | BA
CAPE VERDE | CAYMAN ISLANDS | CHINA | COLOMBIA | COMOROS ISLANDS | COOK ISLANDS | COSTA RICA | CROATIA | CURACAO | CYPRUS | CZECH REPUBLIC | DENMARK |
GRENADA | GUADALCANAL | GUAM | HONDURAS | HONG KONG | HUNGARY | INDIA | INDONESIA | IRAN | IRAQ | IRELAND | ISRAEL | ITALY | JAMAICA | JAPAN | JORDAN | KATM
| MAURITIUS | MEXICO | MICRONESIA | MONACO | MONTENEGRO | MOOREA | MOROCCO | MOZAMBIQUE | MYANMAR | NEPAL | NETHERLANDS | NETHERLANDS ANTILLES |
PUERTO RICO | QATAR | ROMANIA | ROTA | RUSSIA | SAIPAN | SAMOA | SAUDI ARABIA | SCOTLAND | SERBIA | SEYCHELLES | SINGAPORE | SOLOMON ISLANDS | SOUTH AFRICA
| SYRIA | TAHITI | TAIWAN | TANZANIA | TASMANIA | THAILAND | TIBET | TOBAGO | TONGA | TRINIDAD | TUNISIA | TURKEY | TURKMENISTAN | TURKS AND CAICOS ISLANDS

ALGERIA | AMERICAN SAMOA | ANGUILLA | ANTIGUA | ARGENTINA | ARUBA | AUSTRALIA | AUSTRIA | AZERBAIJAN | BAHAMAS | BAHRAIN | BANGLADESH | BARBADOS | BA
CAPE VERDE | CAYMAN ISLANDS | CHINA | COLOMBIA | COMOROS ISLANDS | COOK ISLANDS | COSTA RICA | CROATIA | CURACAO | CYPRUS | CZECH REPUBLIC | DENMARK |
GRENADA | GUADALCANAL | GUAM | HONDURAS | HONG KONG | HUNGARY | INDIA | INDONESIA | IRAN | IRAQ | IRELAND | ISRAEL | ITALY | JAMAICA | JAPAN | JORDAN | KATM
| MAURITIUS | MEXICO | MICRONESIA | MONACO | MONTENEGRO | MOOREA | MOROCCO | MOZAMBIQUE | MYANMAR | NEPAL | NETHERLANDS | NETHERLANDS ANTILLES |
PUERTO RICO | QATAR | ROMANIA | ROTA | RUSSIA | SAIPAN | SAMOA | SAUDI ARABIA | SCOTLAND | SERBIA | SEYCHELLES | SINGAPORE | SOLOMON ISLANDS | SOUTH AFRICA
| SYRIA | TAHITI | TAIWAN | TANZANIA | TASMANIA | THAILAND | TIBET | TOBAGO | TONGA | TRINIDAD | TUNISIA | TURKEY | TURKMENISTAN | TURKS AND CAICOS ISLANDS

ALGERIA | AMERICAN SAMOA | ANGUILLA | ANTIGUA | ARGENTINA | ARUBA | AUSTRALIA | AUSTRIA | AZERBAIJAN | BAHAMAS | BAHRAIN | BANGLADESH | BARBADOS | BA
CAPE VERDE | CAYMAN ISLANDS | CHINA | COLOMBIA | COMOROS ISLANDS | COOK ISLANDS | COSTA RICA | CROATIA | CURACAO | CYPRUS | CZECH REPUBLIC | DENMARK |
GRENADA | GUADALCANAL | GUAM | HONDURAS | HONG KONG | HUNGARY | INDIA | INDONESIA | IRAN | IRAQ | IRELAND | ISRAEL | ITALY | JAMAICA | JAPAN | JORDAN | KATM
| MAURITIUS | MEXICO | MICRONESIA | MONACO | MONTENEGRO | MOOREA | MOROCCO | MOZAMBIQUE | MYANMAR | NEPAL | NETHERLANDS | NETHERLANDS ANTILLES |
PUERTO RICO | QATAR | ROMANIA | ROTA | RUSSIA | SAIPAN | SAMOA | SAUDI ARABIA | SCOTLAND | SERBIA | SEYCHELLES | SINGAPORE | SOLOMON ISLANDS | SOUTH AFRICA
| SYRIA | TAHITI | TAIWAN | TANZANIA | TASMANIA | THAILAND | TIBET | TOBAGO | TONGA | TRINIDAD | TUNISIA | TURKEY | TURKMENISTAN | TURKS AND CAICOS ISLANDS

ALGERIA | AMERICAN SAMOA | ANGUILLA | ANTIGUA | ARGENTINA | ARUBA | AUSTRALIA | AUSTRIA | AZERBAIJAN | BAHAMAS | BAHRAIN | BANGLADESH | BARBADOS | BA
CAPE VERDE | CAYMAN ISLANDS | CHINA | COLOMBIA | COMOROS ISLANDS | COOK ISLANDS | COSTA RICA | CROATIA | CURACAO | CYPRUS | CZECH REPUBLIC | DENMARK |
GRENADA | GUADALCANAL | GUAM | HONDURAS | HONG KONG | HUNGARY | INDIA | INDONESIA | IRAN | IRAQ | IRELAND | ISRAEL | ITALY | JAMAICA | JAPAN | JORDAN | KATM
| MAURITIUS | MEXICO | MICRONESIA | MONACO | MONTENEGRO | MOOREA | MOROCCO | MOZAMBIQUE | MYANMAR | NEPAL | NETHERLANDS | NETHERLANDS ANTILLES |
PUERTO RICO | QATAR | ROMANIA | ROTA | RUSSIA | SAIPAN | SAMOA | SAUDI ARABIA | SCOTLAND | SERBIA | SEYCHELLES | SINGAPORE | SOLOMON ISLANDS | SOUTH AFRICA
| SYRIA | TAHITI | TAIWAN | TANZANIA | TASMANIA | THAILAND | TIBET | TOBAGO | TONGA | TRINIDAD | TUNISIA | TURKEY | TURKMENISTAN | TURKS AND CAICOS ISLANDS

ALGERIA | AMERICAN SAMOA | ANGUILLA | ANTIGUA | ARGENTINA | ARUBA | AUSTRALIA | AUSTRIA | AZERBAIJAN | BAHAMAS | BAHRAIN | BANGLADESH | BARBADOS | BA
CAPE VERDE | CAYMAN ISLANDS | CHINA | COLOMBIA | COMOROS ISLANDS | COOK ISLANDS | COSTA RICA | CROATIA | CURACAO | CYPRUS | CZECH REPUBLIC | DENMARK |
GRENADA | GUADALCANAL | GUAM | HONDURAS | HONG KONG | HUNGARY | INDIA | INDONESIA | IRAN | IRAQ | IRELAND | ISRAEL | ITALY | JAMAICA | JAPAN | JORDAN | KATM
| MAURITIUS | MEXICO | MICRONESIA | MONACO | MONTENEGRO | MOOREA | MOROCCO | MOZAMBIQUE | MYANMAR | NEPAL | NETHERLANDS | NETHERLANDS ANTILLES |
PUERTO RICO | QATAR | ROMANIA | ROTA | RUSSIA | SAIPAN | SAMOA | SAUDI ARABIA | SCOTLAND | SERBIA | SEYCHELLES | SINGAPORE | SOLOMON ISLANDS | SOUTH AFRICA
| SYRIA | TAHITI | TAIWAN | TANZANIA | TASMANIA | THAILAND | TIBET | TOBAGO | TONGA | TRINIDAD | TUNISIA | TURKEY | TURKMENISTAN | TURKS AND CAICOS ISLANDS

ALGERIA | AMERICAN SAMOA | ANGUILLA | ANTIGUA | ARGENTINA | ARUBA | AUSTRALIA | AUSTRIA | AZERBAIJAN | BAHAMAS | BAHRAIN | BANGLADESH | BARBADOS | BA
CAPE VERDE | CAYMAN ISLANDS | CHINA | COLOMBIA | COMOROS ISLANDS | COOK ISLANDS | COSTA RICA | CROATIA | CURACAO | CYPRUS | CZECH REPUBLIC | DENMARK |
GRENADA | GUADALCANAL | GUAM | HONDURAS | HONG KONG | HUNGARY | INDIA | INDONESIA | IRAN | IRAQ | IRELAND | ISRAEL | ITALY | JAMAICA | JAPAN | JORDAN | KATM
| MAURITIUS | MEXICO | MICRONESIA | MONACO | MONTENEGRO | MOOREA | MOROCCO | MOZAMBIQUE | MYANMAR | NEPAL | NETHERLANDS | NETHERLANDS ANTILLES |
PUERTO RICO | QATAR | ROMANIA | ROTA | RUSSIA | SAIPAN | SAMOA | SAUDI ARABIA | SCOTLAND | SERBIA | SEYCHELLES | SINGAPORE | SOLOMON ISLANDS | SOUTH AFRICA
| SYRIA | TAHITI | TAIWAN | TANZANIA | TASMANIA | THAILAND | TIBET | TOBAGO | TONGA | TRINIDAD | TUNISIA | TURKEY | TURKMENISTAN | TURKS AND CAICOS ISLANDS